Praise for *Talent to Tri*

"Moving from being talented to the elite levels is the toughest challenge for any young athlete. The lessons in this brilliant book from those who've been there, done it, faced challenges, faced fear, overcome obstacles and achieved their dreams makes it an invaluable resource".

~ Sir Ben Ainslie CBE: 4 × Olympic Champion,
11 × World Champion; Sailing

"Having watched Amy train every day for years, there is nobody better qualified to describe what it takes to make it in sport. She was relentless & became the very best".

~ David Flatman: Saracens, Bath and England,
Rugby Union, Broadcaster

"Amy has written a fantastic blueprint for young athletes to learn from. Her experiences, mixed with those of so many other elite performers make this book an absolute treasure trove of advice".

~ Kate Grey: Paralympian, World Championships Medallist,
Broadcaster, Mentor; Swimming

"Amy Williams knows what it takes to win. As an Olympian – & an Olympic champion no less – her experience, insight and opinion carries great value for anyone who wants to follow in her footsteps. As part of Great Britain's skeleton team she has been part of one of this country's most successful sports teams, producing serial winners Games after Games".

Mike Hay, Chef de Mission (Sochi 2014 Olympic Winter Games)

"Amy Williams has written a book which will be as invaluable to young athletes and sports people as it will be to the parents & carers who nurture them. Her insight and experience has been carefully distilled into proper take away nuggets of advice, warnings and learnings from her exemplary career as a gold medal winning Olympian & from the observations of other sports men and women she has witnessed being successful and making mistakes along the way. You will want to thank her when you have read it".

~ Gabby Logan MBE: Sports Broadcaster,
Former International Rhythmic Gymnast

"Having trained from a very early age I can appreciate that there are certain times growing up when there are added pressures in a young athlete's life. Balancing education, social life and activities, family commitments & training are major mountains to overcome. It is understandable that this is the time when most aspiring elite athletes lose their way and are likely to get side-tracked. Amy has the experience and expertise at the highest level of elite sport and has created a very credible "go to" to provide support and guidance across a range of topics from mindset to preparation to setbacks. I am sure it will help lots of up & coming talent".

~ Victoria Pendleton CBE: Double Olympic Champion,
Multiple World Champion; Track Cycling

"Anyone involved with any sport will benefit enormously from this book. **Talent to Triumph** is relentlessly practical, you simply can't fail to be inspired & educated by Amy & the incredible list of contributors".

~ Helen Skelton: Broadcaster; Blue Peter, Countryfile, BBC Swimming

"Most young people in sport take years to build the required knowledge for success through (often difficult) experiences, sometimes this can be too late. Amy has written a book that means a reader can learn everything they'd need to know in an instant, highly recommended".

~ Sir Clive Woodward OBE: World Cup Winning Head Coach;
England Rugby Union, Head Coach; British and Irish Lions,
Director of Football; Southampton FC, Director of Sport;
British Olympic Association

"We believe that all young people should benefit from the life changing benefits of sport & that they can find their passion & interest by exploring as many sports as possible. Amy explores some of the key concepts in helping anyone who has the determination to excel and fulfil their potential. Through her invaluable insights Amy helps us understand the decisions and opportunities that lie ahead".

~ The Youth Sport Trust

TALENT
TO
TRIUMPH

AMY WILLIAMS MBE

TALENT

TO

TRIUMPH

HOW ATHLETES TURN POTENTIAL
INTO HIGH PERFORMANCE

First published in 2021 by Sequoia Books

ISBN
Print: 9781914110092
EPUB: 9781914110108

A CIP record for this book is available from the British Library

Library of Congress Cataloguing-In-Publication Data
Name: Amy Williams, author
Title: Talent to Triumph: How Athletes Turn Potential Into High Performance / Amy Williams
Description: 1st Edition, Sequoia Books UK 2021
Print: 9781914110092
EPUB: 9781914110108

Library of Congress Control Number: 2021916767

Print and Electronic production managed by Deanta Global

Cover designed by Kelly Miller

Book Tribute

To my two gorgeous, wonderful boys, Oscar and Alfie. You are the reason I have written this book. I want to inspire you both to find a passion that you love, to dream as big as you want and to show you that you can achieve anything that you put your mind to.

Contents

About the Author

Amy Williams became the first ever female in Great Britain to win an Olympic Gold medal in the winter sport of skeleton. At her debut Winter Olympic Games in 2010, Amy claimed Team GB's only gold medal of the Games. In winning Gold, she became Britain's first solo Winter Olympics champion in 30 years and the first female individual gold medallist for 58 years. In 2010, she was awarded an MBE for services to sport and, in the same year, became only the fifth person since the Second World War to be made an Honorary Freeman of the City of Bath. The University of Bath also awarded her an honorary degree of Doctor of Laws in June 2017.

After retiring from the sport in spring of 2012, Amy has done a lot of other works, including television, public appearances and motivational speaking. Amy has presented on BBC's Ski Sunday and has joined the BBC Sport commentary team for their coverage at winter sports events, including the Sochi 2014 and Pyeongchang 2018 Olympics. She presented on the Gadget Show for 3 years and took part in TV challenge shows such as Alone in the Wild, 71 Degrees North and Tour de Celeb. Since 2018 she has been a part of the ITV presenting team covering the Isle of Man TT Races.

Amy's passion for fitness is still burning strong. She now runs her own personal training business, helping others achieve their fitness and health goals, creating a motivating and inspiring space to workout.

She is a sought-after speaker talking to children and businesses, from school prize giving to corporate events, conferences or team building days.

Amy is a role model for showing that nothing is impossible if you work hard, having a huge amount of determination, perseverance and inner strength. She loves telling her Olympic story in a motivational and inspiring way, sharing her tips to achieve those 1% differences to achieve high performance.

Amy is an ambassador for the Dame Kelly Holmes Trust and has spoken for the Youth Sport Trust and Sports Aid among others.

She is on the British Skeleton Team Committee and is an athlete mentor. She has also been to several summer and winter Youth Olympics with Team GB as their athlete mentor.

Acknowledgements

It's been an amazing experience writing this book, revisiting my old skeleton memories and those moments I had almost forgotten, bringing them back to life for others to learn from, share with and for me to hopefully help the next generation of young athletes, who, just like myself all those years ago, had a passion and dream to achieve and be their very best.

To win my Olympic Gold medal, to hold it in my hands for the first time while I stood on top of the podium in front of the whole world, Wow Wow Wow, I knew that finally all of those days of hard training, the pain, the sweat, pushing my body to the limit was 100% worth it.

I want to say a massive thank you to everyone who has helped me make this book happen. To Andrew Peart, my wonderful publisher, and to Sequoia Books for liking the idea and supporting me the whole way through. To all of the contributors who have given their wise words of wisdom, their stories and quotes – all willing to inspire and help the next budding athlete. You have enriched this book considerably. Thank you all.

However, none of it would have been possible without my loved ones beside me. Most importantly my family, Simon and Ruth my brother and sister, growing up so close, always playing, pushing each other and supporting one another.

My mum and dad. A million thanks to you both. You are the ones who endlessly drove me up and down the country in those early years to athletics competitions, then at those 3 a.m. mornings to the airport so I could catch those early flights for skeleton training. I'm sorry for the lack of sleep and the stress I put you through as I competed in the slightly mad sport of skeleton! Your unconditional love and support meant I was able to follow my dreams and achieve my goal. In both your words every time you said goodbye at each airport, "Just do your best, God Bless You, we love you". I love you both so much. This book is for you.

Finally, to my husband, Craig. My best friend and soul mate. You are there next to me every day, always inspiring me to achieve more and inspire our boys. I hope this book makes you proud.

1 Selecting Your Sport

Selecting your sport is potentially a more complex process than you might first imagine. This chapter is all about what goes into the decisions that may be the difference between making it as an elite athlete and giving up sport altogether. We'll look at elements like the need to love a sport, your natural abilities, transitioning from one event to another, talent identification and keeping an open mind.

My story is a good example of the varied journey that an athlete might have to take if they want to achieve the highest levels of success. Mine was like a lot of people's early experiences of sport. I was doing a lot of school sports, I was pretty much the kid that did everything: there was netball, hockey and athletics. When I started sixth form we did some swimming competitions and a little bit of tennis as well. I got a lot out of doing a variety of sports, mainly as it helped me decide which was the right one for me at that time. I took a particular shine to athletics, I felt like I was pretty good at it, so I joined the local club in Bath and continued progressing throughout my teenage years.

TRY SEVERAL SPORTS

For many people including myself, rather than specifically selecting a sport, it's often the case that the sport will eventually select you. I was living in Bath, which is the home of modern pentathlon, so I ended giving that a go when I was around 19. I remember seeing the posters of the 2000 Olympic team featuring Stephanie Cook and Georgina Harland around the university where my dad worked. It was a similar story with skeleton, it just happened to be in Bath and I was willing to give it a go. You might have a particularly good cricket team nearby, or access to a local swimming pool. If you have good facilities or there's a particular tradition for a sport close to home, then give them a try; you just never know which might end up suiting you perfectly. There's always an element of luck, but if you chat to the right people at the right time, you'll give yourself a much better chance of finding your sport. Likewise, if your family are involved in a sport and you grew up around it, you might find yourself immersed in it from an early age. Ultimately, there is a lot of routes to discover your sport, give yourself time, create your opportunities and go from there.

If you're doing a lot of different sports then you'll start to see if you have natural talent for some over others. For me, I noticed that sprinting was something I was consistently good at. This led to the skeleton coaches seeing the raw materials of someone who had that initial burst over 30 metres, good core strength, body awareness and coordination from riding horses at a young age that they were looking for. In other words, I found my own natural ability and was able to match it to one of the many sports I was trying.

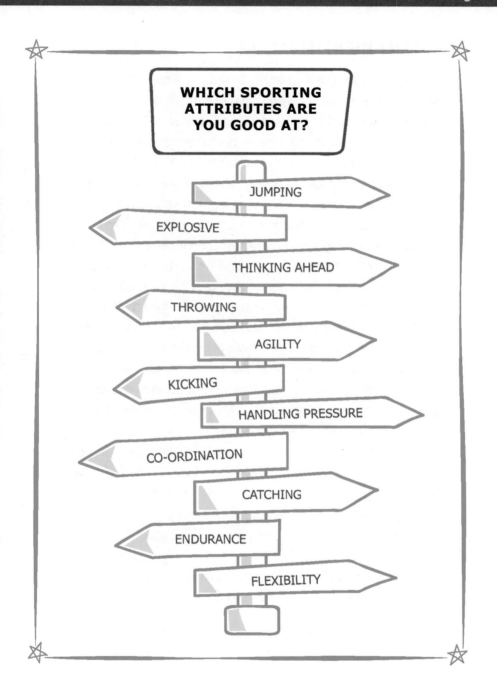

TALENT IDENTIFICATION

This is very much the way British Skeleton use talent identification now. If someone has that raw speed over the first 30 metres, then that's a good initial foundation to work with. This might get around twenty young athletes onto the high performance programme from a group of approximately 500. At this stage the coaches would start looking at a wider variety of elements like explosive power, reaction times, the athlete's mentality, commitment, ability to learn and such things. You start to develop a much bigger profile of someone when they get on the ice for the first time. How do they deal with setbacks? How do they deal with crashing? How do they deal with the fear? How do they deal with being away from home? Do they maintain positivity in the face of adversity? There was an occasion several years ago when we took a group of young skeleton athletes down to spend a weekend with the Royal Marines to take them through some of their training. They were set into two teams, given some tasks to do and generally put under a little bit of pressure. It was really fascinating to see who was better at listening to instructions, who could perform under pressure, who could remember things and repeat them later when tired, how was everyone's attitude throughout their time there, who stood back and was more timid, who dealt with the physical challenges of the assault course (while being shouted at by the Marines!), who was willing to help their teammates, who gave up early. This gave the coaches a lot of information on who might have the physical and mental ingredients to excel.

Some people will realise quickly that a particular sport or a particular lifestyle just isn't the right one for them, others thrive in it. There's no right or wrong to either of these outcomes, in my eyes it's always a positive that you've tried something. If it works out, fantastic, if not, then you've made the decision for the right reasons, now use this knowledge and experience to find a sport that suits you much better. The early stages of elite sport can be quite cut-throat, but always use it as a learning experience. I spent many years with dreams of being a 400-metre runner, but as it turned out, I was far more suited to a 30-metre burst of speed (clearly there's another 370 metres in my first sport, which were a little far for me!) which took me to a very different event. It took trying several of them and matching my abilities (with commitment and dedication) to one that I eventually found worked for me. Don't be disheartened or see it as a rejection, take the positives from whatever experience you've had. Just because one sport may not be right for you, another may well be.

"Note to Self"

"Never give up trying.

It's better to try lots

of different sports

and fail, then never

try at all".

If you're inclined to research further (I'd strongly encourage you to do so) then there's a lot of information on how different talent identification programmes work. The UK sport website (www.uksport.gov.uk) is a great place to start. They outline how everything works and how you can get involved:

"Our talent recruitment and confirmation programmes are multi-phased. Campaigns start with a talent search, either with the general public or within the sport's community. This involves athletes submitting an application form to UK Sport for consideration. After careful analysis, successful applicants are invited to the phase 1 testing events hosted in various locations around the country."

Similarly, there's an organisation called TASS (Talented Athlete Scholarship Scheme) that works with talented young athletes on balancing their sporting journey with their academic studies as well. They're well worth looking into.

These schemes that come in various forms have produced some exceptional talent over the years. There's Team GB skeleton athletes Laura Deas and Lizzy Yarnold who were part of the "Girls for Gold" scheme run by UK Sport, both of whom came from different sports. Double Olympic champion Helen Glover started rowing as part of the "Sporting Giants" initiative, as did Rio 2016 silver medallist Vicky Thornley (a former equestrian competitor before switching to rowing). Lutalo Muhammed won an Olympic medal, having previously applied to the "Fighting Chance" talent ID campaign among many other stories from many different competitors.

These are just a fraction of the success stories from talent identification. I find it so interesting that so many of our athletes found success having moved from one sport to another. Never feel like rejection from one sport means the end of your sporting journey, you just might not have matched your ability to the right event yet.

ATHLETE IN FOCUS

Laura Deas –
Olympic Bronze Medallist Pyeongchang 2018, Skeleton

The idea of a formal "Talent ID" scheme is pretty well known now, but back in 2008 when I applied to the UK Sport scheme "Girls4Gold", it was the first time that such a thing had been done on a nationwide scale. I was really intrigued to see how sports scientists would be able to tell what I was naturally suited to through just a few physical tests, and also how possible it would really be to transition and fast track into elite level competition in a completely different sport. It's fair to say I felt really nervous about trialling in 2008 but also really excited to see if I could potentially be world class in one of the sports on offer. I gave all the tests my full effort on the day with no idea if I was doing any of them well!

When I got a letter through the post saying that I had been invited to try skeleton at the University of Bath, I was really excited! Skeleton seemed like a really risky and extreme sport which was what I was used to with my current sport of horse riding, so I felt like it was something I might naturally take to. At first around 200 girls were asked to try pushing a sled at the special push track facility in Bath, and over the course of the winter and a few training sessions, that number was reduced to around 8. This tiny group of us were then taken to Norway to try the sport out on ice and see how we got on.

Until getting to Norway, the emphasis had really been on the physical aspect of accelerating the sled through the push start and the technique of the load, but now everything had changed – it was about learning how to drive a sled down a narrow, twisting ice chute at up to

80 mph. This was a massive and unique challenge for everyone and I quickly realised that as well as being taught how to slide, we were also being tested on who could learn the quickest and also who would be mentally and physically strong enough to keep doing something scary over and over again until we improved.

I think this is where my background in horse riding really helped me. I might not have been the most physically talented of the girls but I was very well practised at putting myself in potentially scary situations and keeping a cool, rational mind. When you ride horses you understand that you are never 100% in control, and so you develop an ability to accept injury risks, predict what might be about to happen and also react to sudden changes with a plan B. I also seemed more willing than some of the others to put myself through physical pain such as hitting walls repeatedly, slamming my chin on the ice under the G force, and of course the extreme cold!

It was a really tough experience, and along the way plenty of the girls decided it wasn't for them! In the end I think my willingness to step into the unknown in order to learn was what helped me be success-ful. My coach at the time gave me some advice which I have never forgotten: "control the controllables". This reminds me not only of not to waste energy on the things I can't change (for example, wishing a really difficult corner could be changed – of course this isn't going to happen!), but also to have a really good plan for the things I can control (for example, my steering plan, how I set my sled up, how much sleep I get). This simple phrase helps me check in with what is actually going to make a positive difference to my sliding performance every time.

To give you more of a direct picture of what talent ID schemes are all about, I asked **Danny Holdcroft, Head of Performance for the BBSA** (British Bobsleigh and Skeleton Association) to share some thoughts:

What's the profile of the athlete you'd be looking for, with regards both physical and mental abilities?

It's far too easy just to select potential talent on physical attributes and we'd hope that the days where you are too small or don't fit what we are looking for physically are long gone. Of course, as a sport we have physical parameters but these are set at the minimum criteria. We back our coaching ability and innovative mindset to develop high performance and we place a strong emphasis on the character traits that are essential if athletes are to excel in our sport. We spend a lot of time looking at how individuals handle different situations – their ability to problem solve; how they adapt to working within a group for certain tasks but on their own for others; and how they react to being placed under time pressure. These elements have a crucial role to play in an athlete reaching elite level.

How should an athlete prepare for a selection programme?

Like with everything where there is an assessment, you should prepare yourself as best you possibly can by understanding what the programme will consist of and what will help show yourself in the best light. Preparation is a key part of elite sport and being fully prepared early on in a selection process is a good indication for us as to how a person may apply themselves later on. That being said, assessments are really about us understanding you as a person, so you need to be yourself, otherwise any character trait you are hiding will most likely show in the future. It's important to be honest to yourself and not be afraid to expose your whole character.

How do you go about testing the athletes for the above traits?

Physical measures are easy to collect but we use a lot of pyscho-social profiling to help understand character traits. However, experience tells us the best assessment tool is simply direct contact time with individuals. Engaging in conversation and interacting in a one-on-one and group basis is hugely informative.

What should an athlete expect when they join the programme?

If a high-performance programme is set up correctly, it should stretch you and take you away from your comfort zone. High performance is about pushing boundaries and we are really proud of our ability to do that successfully cycle after cycle.

Do the successful athletes (those that reach the GB team) have traits in common that puts them above others?

Yes. They are all driven to succeed and focussed on what they need to do to achieve their goals. When required, they have a selfish trait to pursue excellence.

LOVE FOR AN EVENT CAN GROW OVER TIME

Talent identification schemes have brought a lot of positives to British sport. They've also highlighted some interesting points regarding your own reasons for choosing your event. You might often hear the advice "find a sport you love". While this is nice and I'd be the first person to encourage everyone to enjoy sports, there are certain realities to elite competition that means you might be more gifted in one over another, so think carefully about this. As you'll read later in the book, there were elements to skeleton that weren't always enjoyable for me, particularly in my early years in the sport. Yes, there's the fear, the danger and the being away from home all the time, but I also hated the cold! I remember when a talent ID initiative for the British Beach Volleyball team came to Bath University. I thought, "yes please"; Beach volleyball sounds fun and I'll happily spend my days on warm beaches, count me in. That was until I realised that the main prerequisite for the talent ID was being over 6 feet tall. My 5'8 stature sadly put a premature end to my glittering beach volleyball career before it even began.

"Note to Self"

"Sometimes your journey may feel 1 step forward, 2 steps back. But have FAITH in the process and your ability".

You might have been concentrating on one sport that you've loved since you were 10 years old. If your natural physiology doesn't suit that sport, there's a good chance that you'll only reach a certain level in it until you realise you might not be tall enough, you might not be fast enough or strong enough. Young athletes often reach a crucial point when learning they might not be able to achieve the elite levels no matter what they do. This isn't down to your commitment or your dedication, it's down to your competitors having a huge advantage by being naturally taller, faster or stronger. At this stage, too many young athletes just become disheartened and can quit sport altogether. Or they can think like me, like Laura Deas, like Lizzy Yarnold, they start thinking about which sports *do* suit them. You can rest assured that there *will* be a sport out there that you'd enjoy advantages over others and one where your commitment and dedication can take you much further based on your natural abilities.

> "DESIRE, DREAM, DEDICATION, DISCIPLINE, DIRECTION AND DETERMINATION. ALL THE D'S THAT WILL LEAD YOU TO SPORTING SUCCESS".

This can lead to more decisions for talented young athletes. Yes, you might have been lucky enough to have a sport with good facilities near where you grow up, but if someone tells you you're physiologically talented for track cycling, do you need to move up to Manchester like Laura Kenny did to be close to the centre of excellence there? For me, the passion of wanting to be really good at a sport outweighed the need to stay near home or the need to be immediately and consistently in love with a sport. This is a decision you might need to think carefully about. Ultimately, I slowly fell in love with skeleton. Even though I may have initially preferred the thought of beaches to ice, volleying a ball to being terrified of crashing, or running around a 400-metre track to speeding down an ice track at 90 mph I chose to pursue a sport that I was naturally gifted at. My enjoyment of skeleton came from the knowledge that I had genuine potential, the knowledge that I could improve quickly, I could learn the tracks, learn better technique, get stronger and get faster, all in the context that I knew I was training hard in a sport that suited me. On top of this, I started developing friendships and I appreciated that I had an amazing opportunity here. All of these factors started mixing together over time and I realised that I actually do really quite like this. All of these are factors that can happen in any sport, not just the one that might have been your first love.

"WHEN AN OPPORTUNITY AND CHANCE COMES YOUR WAY, THEN SAY YES, GIVE IT A GO, YOU WILL NEVER REGRET TRYING".

I then found there were increasingly times when I thought that skeleton felt amazing, despite my early misgivings. I'd complete a run down a track that felt really smooth, that was fun, and that was exhilarating. I didn't think about anything else, I just slid and I had these feelings of amazing enjoyment. These feelings can grow over time. I remember the first time I had the experience of pure joy with skeleton. It was at a place called Igls, in Innsbruck, Austria. Igls is quite a gentle track, but very fast at the bottom, it's a "pushers" track, so the sprinters like me were more suited to it and it never felt as dangerous as some of the other tracks. Innsbruck is stunning, we were there around Christmas time so we'd visit the Christmas markets. Everything about the environment and the experience was wonderful.

It took some time for me to fall in love with the sport, but it happened. Don't rule out other sports that might suit you more than those that in the short term you might have more immediate enjoyment. It doesn't necessarily have to be the sport itself that you're completely in love with. It might be elements of it that can come together to make you fall in love with a new sport over time.

KEEP AN OPEN MIND

The key to selecting what might eventually become your chosen sport is to maintain an open mind. Don't rush to a decision; don't put yourself in any kind of "box" that defines who and what you might do. Yes, there are certain realities that if your dream is to play basketball in the NBA, then you're probably going to need to be very tall but that's an extreme example. I look at myself and think that while I showed some aptitude for sprinting as a young athlete, I don't think my physiology was so extremely weighted to those fast twitch fibres that I couldn't have also explored being an 800-metre runner as well. I think I had a reasonably balanced physiology and could have gone in either direction of long or short distance. This is also the case at the elite levels. Think about this when you watch a middle or long distance race on TV, where you'll hear the commentators talking of certain athletes having a better sprint finish, or others that prefer to lead from the front.

ELITE INSIGHT

Brian Ashton MBE –
Former Head Coach, England and Ireland Rugby Union

What do young people who play sport experience? If allowed to be themselves and explore the endless possibilities of their environments, a great deal.

Enjoyment and an affinity which can last a lifetime, learning and behavioural traits which are transferable to life outside of sport.

The fondest memories I have of my formative years are "street play": in all its forms. FREEDOM, FLEXIBILITY, FEARLESSNESS, FURIOUS, FUN. No adults to interfere, enabled us to develop elements of self-sufficiency, management and improvement.

In the current world of data, analysis and interfering coaching, it is still critical that we allow kids to be kids with appropriate help and guidance. Help them to become joyful people.

In the often called "pressurised environments" (an overused phrase) of current top-level sport we must still retain the FUN element of our childhood.

Only recently one of the greatest Rugby players the world has seen, former All Black, Dan Carter said. "The game has changed pretty quickly. It's faster, the players are stronger. There's so much more science. *But you need fun; you need characters*. If it gets too serious it's going to get stale".

A powerful message for us all involved at any level.

Most sporting disciplines have so many elements to them that mean just being naturally gifted in one of these isn't enough to think you're going to be an automatic champion or that you know precisely what your chosen sport should be. Someone may well have those slow twitch fibres needed for a longer distance race, but how many times have we seen someone else sprint past them on the final bend of a middle distance race? For me in skeleton, yes I needed the initial burst of speed for the push start, but I also needed a lot more besides. I needed mental toughness, extreme coordination, body control, the ability to retain complex information, the ability to cope with fear, the ability to lie in the perfect aerodynamic position on the sled. Just having one element of talent isn't enough to define you or which event you might ultimately choose. I've seen many examples of extremely fast, high level sprinters try out skeleton or try out bobsleigh and find that raw speed just isn't enough.

I was lucky in that I felt I had natural ability beyond the raw speed of the push start, the trick is to harness that ability with dedicated training to build on it. There's old footage of me on a sled where I looked more like a scorpion than a skeleton athlete in the perfect flat position. But ultimately, with work, I had the genetics to work through it and get to where I needed to be, this is because I selected the right sport for me. This is also where training from other sports can really work in your favour. I see Lizzy Yarnold's power on the push start, much of which would have come from her years of heptathlon training. Laura Deas has phenomenal core strength, body control and bravery from her days in cross country equestrian. She also has a high aptitude for learning the nuances of ice tracks, which would have been helped by learning complex cross-country courses quickly and effectively. Rebecca Romero is another incredible example of how high achievement in one sport can lead to success in another. Rebecca won world championships and Olympic medals in rowing, before going to even greater success in cycling, winning the 2008 Olympic individual pursuit gold medal, following on from two golds at the UCI track cycling world championships.

Try not to pigeonhole yourself at too young an age. You may well find yourself frustrated that you aren't achieving what you feel like your commitment, dedication and enthusiasm deserve. This isn't the moment to give up on sport. This is the moment to give yourself credit for being committed, dedicated and enthusiastic and use those traits towards a sport that you might find is much more suited to you. My reality is that if I'd have continued down the path of wanting to be a 400-metre runner, I simply wouldn't have made it, I didn't have the required natural ability. I tried modern pentathlon, which went pretty well, I also tried another sport that I'd barely even known existed. Turns out that was a pretty good choice.

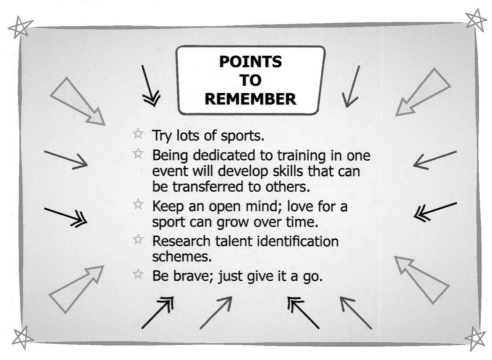

POINTS TO REMEMBER

☆ Try lots of sports.
☆ Being dedicated to training in one event will develop skills that can be transferred to others.
☆ Keep an open mind; love for a sport can grow over time.
☆ Research talent identification schemes.
☆ Be brave; just give it a go.

2 Barriers

Barriers are an inevitable part of every athlete's journey to success. They appear in many different forms and at any stage of your sporting journey. Your barriers will often feel unique to you and in many cases, they will be.

The purpose of this chapter is to give you examples of some of the barriers you might face and provide some coping strategies to help you overcome as many as possible. I'll explain some of the many barriers that I faced, how I was able to respond to them, how you can adapt, what you can control, how you maintain momentum in the face of adversity and the things I wish I'd known when I was a teenage athlete that would have better prepared me. We'll also take some advice from other elite athletes who became experts at beating the odds in overcoming both minor bumps in the road and seemingly unbeatable obstacles.

The good news is that a high proportion of barriers can be managed, overcome or, even better, transformed into advantages.

FACILITIES AND EQUIPMENT

Let's start by looking at facilities and equipment (or lack thereof). Different sports clearly require different tools and different environments. This means a lot of potential barriers if your chosen sport lacks in this department. If as a young person I'd had a burning desire to be a footballer, a cross country runner, a cyclist or an open water swimmer, then facilities would most likely have been less of a problem than they were when I decided on skeleton as my event!

Britain is a country that doesn't have an ice track, so it's fair to say that facilities were indeed against me. Looking back now I think how crazy it might have been to have chosen a sport with very little prospect of regular high-quality training at a dedicated facility. The only British-based set-up I had access to was the push track at the University of Bath. This was essentially a train track on rubber matting to practice the sprint start, on the face of it not entirely ideal.

Comparing this to a German skeleton athlete, who has access to three world-class tracks in their country, along with the Canadians and Americans who have ice push houses to practice their sprint starts pushing real ice sleds on the ice. There'd be a temptation to think the inequality in facilities makes it pointless to even think about reaching elite levels.

Not so.

I didn't realise it at the time, but the silver lining to this apparent cloud was a mentality forming in me that in British winter sports you learn to *control the controllables*, because you have to. You learn very quickly to take what seems like a barrier and use it to your advantage. I believe that one of the reasons British skeleton has enjoyed so much success in the recent past is that we've learned to make dramatic improvements in all those other tiny areas, unaffected by lack of facilities. No ice track didn't mean we couldn't aim to get better at everything else, better than every country in the world, in fact. We learn how to get good fast!

Yes, the German athletes had fantastic access to immaculate tracks, to the point where they could and did, become exceptional on those tracks. But could we in Britain develop the best warm-up routines? Could we learn the best recovery strategies? Could we prepare our sleds in the best way possible? Could we put in place a philosophy whereby we could learn every track in the world in the greatest detail and fast? The answer to these is yes, we could and we did. I always felt that if I can get down the most basic push-start track on a rickety old sled like I did in my early years, I was still putting the building blocks in place to become a good skeleton athlete. If I can get *that* sled down a track faster and faster, then by the time I eventually had access to a good sled and an actual ice track I'd be at an advantage over the other athletes who always had the best equipment and full access to ice tracks their whole career.

FOCUS ON WHAT YOU DO HAVE, NOT WHAT YOU DON'T. PERFECT YOUR SKILLS WITH THE EQUIPMENT AND FACILITIES AVAILABLE

I'm writing this book in the midst of the horrendous global 2020/21 coronavirus pandemic, where lockdowns have become the norm. A skeleton athlete I mentor has said he's far more consistent in lockdown, he's done things he wouldn't normally do with gyms available, he's stretched far more, he's done more yoga and now feels like he's the best athlete he's ever been. He's now in an incredible routine, he's doing all his rehab more consistently, he's doing the smaller preparation work that were normally overlooked pre-lockdown, precisely because he doesn't have the perfect set up.

Wasting time worrying about lack of equipment or facilities or anything else outside of your control is just that, a waste. Learn the mindset that other athletes might have perfect facilities, but they haven't learned to do all the smaller things in the same detail as you, they haven't developed the resiliency that you have, they haven't learned an adaptable mindset. You have, because you've had to.

A similar theme to controlling the controllables (which you'll hear a lot about) is to **think outside the box**. The pandemic has put up unprecedented facility and equipment-based barriers for athletes across all sports. Gyms have been closed for long periods, training areas are shut down and access to all of the usual things an athlete would otherwise consider essential have all but stopped. Despite the difficulties this has created, it's also given a great insight into the mindset of elite athletes in how they overcome barriers, think outside the box and why they've moved from good to great.

Another of the current skeleton athletes I mentor couldn't get to a gym, but her dad works for a car company. He gave her a steel bar, welded old car tyres to each end, then using their green garden bins, hey presto they have a fully functioning squat rack. Holly Bradshaw, the GB Olympic pole vaulter, showed on social media that when she couldn't train with a full-length pole, she used a shorter one with a tin of baked beans taped to the end to replicate the weight. I've seen for myself, as a qualified personal trainer while teaching my online zoom fitness classes and discovering that wine bottles or rucksacks filled with books are the perfect weight for people to be doing tricep extensions. You might not have a perfect athletics track near you, but you can find a hill to do hill sprints, getting stronger than those running on flat tracks.

Lack of equipment or facilities doesn't have to be a reason to hold you back, see them as excellent lessons for you in adaptability, resilience, determination and persistence, none of which you'd be learning if everything was constantly perfect.

We'd all hope to never see a pandemic again, but the lessons on how athletes think outside the box and make the very best of what's available are a great example for you as a teenage athlete to use for your whole career.

ELITE INSIGHT

Dame Sarah Storey DBE –
Multiple Paralympic, World and European Champion; Swimming and Cycling

I was working in a very positive environment, where the word "can't" didn't exist and a process driven approach meant nothing was insurmountable. I think this has helped shape my life outside of sport too, I am always eager to look for a solution, which helps create a positive mindset and gives me motivation that whatever the challenge there is a way to move forward. I also think this builds confidence in an individual too, if you feel in control and capable then you feel confident you can tackle even the most difficult times.

YOUR PERSONALITY IS NOT A BARRIER

Facilities barriers aren't of course the only ones you'll face. Sometimes your own perception of yourself has the potential to hold you back. We'll discuss mindset techniques later in the book, but for the purpose of this chapter, think about how you see your own personality and whether you think it's something that drives you forward or holds you back. From my experience, there is no perfect personality to strive towards in your quest to reach higher sporting goals. All personalities can achieve great things. I'll let you into a secret: I'm shy!

Shyness is a barrier that many young athletes face and was most certainly one that I experienced as a teenager. There's a false tendency to feel like all the best athletes are supremely confident and naturally outgoing people. This isn't me at all and I often wondered whether this would hold me back from my reaching the elite levels of my sport.

I think back to my early days in skeleton after I'd first shown some potential. It was 2002 and I was invited to join a big army ice camp for 2 weeks in Lillehammer, Norway. I'd only just turned 18 and was a naturally introverted character. I had to take a plane, then several trains across Europe to get there, it was freezing cold, miserable and we were staying in these tiny wooden huts that weren't exactly the lap of luxury. I remember seeing the big, powerful, confident army girls on the bobsleigh team, feeling very self-conscious as a much smaller skeleton athlete. "What on earth am I doing here?" I asked myself on more than one occasion. Then of course my lack of self-assuredness reared its head even more so when the actual business of skeleton training began. The first time I went down the ice track I secretly cried at the bottom. The second and third times? You guessed it, more tears. The physicality of sliding, the emotion, the fear, the unknown. You're crashing, you're hitting the sides, you're covered head to toe in bruises, not to mention you're hundreds of miles away from home, you're shy and you lack self-belief. I didn't exactly love it.

Several things helped me keep going after this camp: first, the knowledge that despite my shyness, I stuck at it and completed the training, secondly, that I thought "hang on a minute, I could be really good at this sport" and thirdly, perhaps most importantly, that I'd started to learn coping strategies to make the most of the way that *my* personality is. It would have been next to useless for someone to say to me "you need to lose the shyness". I'd started to realise that shyness isn't something that's going to hold me back, it's something that I can control, something that I can work with and something that I can thrive with.

Fast forward a few years and even at the Olympics I was never the most outgoing athlete. I had, however, learned to develop a level of internal self-confidence that made me unrecognizable from the self-doubting, terrified 18-year-old in Lillehammer. Here's how I did it and more importantly, how you can do it too.

I never looked at ways in which I could make myself less shy, that just wouldn't have suited me. I put more emphasis on working with it and being the best I could be alongside it. I knew I wasn't the type of person to be out socialising all the time with everyone on the team, so I brought my little portable DVD player with my favourite films (clearly this was in a world without too many iPads and mobile phones, but you get the point!) and I brought tons of books. I was creating my own happy place at the end of the busy day, once the sliding, training, video feedback and sled work had been done. For me this switch off time meant I could go into another world and forget about the day. It was really important to me (especially after a really bad day on the ice). I also became really great friends with some of the athletes from other nations, mainly those with similar personalities to me. If we ever had a spare few hours on a day off then we would meet up and chat over a hot chocolate in any coffee shop or hotel lobby we could find.

What is my default behaviour?

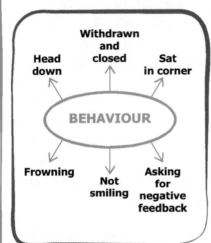

BEHAVIOUR

Withdrawn and closed

Head down

Sat in corner

Frowning

Not smiling

Asking for negative feedback

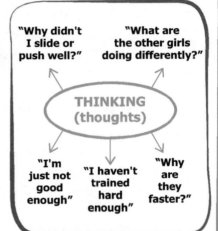

THINKING (thoughts)

"Why didn't I slide or push well?"

"What are the other girls doing differently?"

"I'm just not good enough"

"I haven't trained hard enough"

"Why are they faster?"

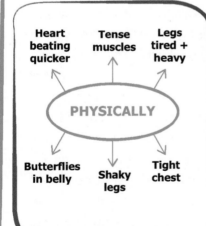

PHYSICALLY

Heart beating quicker

Tense muscles

Legs tired + heavy

Butterflies in belly

Shaky legs

Tight chest

FEELING (emotions)

Upset

Scared

Panicky

Fear of failure

Crying

Deflated

YOUR TURN

What is my default behaviour?

BEHAVIOUR

THINKING
(thoughts)

PHYSICALLY

FEELING
(emotions)

Travelling is a big part of sport (particularly winter sports) and I was always really emotional saying goodbye to my parents. At the airport my dad would just give me a hug and say "oh just do your best". We didn't have the internet, so instead, I had a little pay as you go phone that was 50 p a text message. I scratched off a little call card in North America and tried to rush a 3-minute phone conversation. My mum would post me letters in advance of where I was arriving, so I'd arrive at a little bed and breakfast and there'd already be a letter waiting for me. She'd never say a great deal, just "hope you're alright and settled in, do your best, it's gonna be fine". This was really important for me; as simple as it was, it really helped me feel happy away from home and family. I would bring my own pillow from home, a travel kettle, tea bags and a pot of honey (I'm a honey monster – when I was too nervous to eat breakfast, I knew I could always eat some honey on toast!). Having home comforts around you and making yourself feel happy in your environment (your hotel room) can make a big difference to how you feel every day and therefore have a positive effect on your performance.

Ultimately, I was learning that in order to get the best out of myself I needed to be comfortable. The more experience I gained from travelling to competitions around the world, the more I realised what made me enjoy the experience and feel relaxed, so I could concentrate on the sport, not on the worry, as I did in Lillehammer all those years before. Whether you're naturally introverted, naturally outgoing or somewhere in between, you can be successful in sport. Learn what makes you happy and build this into your routine.

BODY IMAGE

Your perception of yourself isn't just limited to your personality. Over recent years we've seen lots of athletes across different sports discuss the issue of body image.

Body image (for both males and females) may well be something you've thought about or are currently thinking about. In its most serious forms it can lead to many negative consequences including eating disorders, low self-esteem, quitting sport and mental health problems. My first and absolutely most important piece of advice is that if you're experiencing issues around body image, please seek help from a qualified professional. Don't keep it to yourself, there's a great deal of help out there for you and you're most certainly not alone.

There's now so much analysis on performance on a weekly or monthly basis, something I didn't have as much in my days as an athlete. The increased use of science has brought along many benefits, but also a microscopic level of data on everything connected to your body. This brings about a lot more pressure on those who may not feel comfortable and experience feelings of vulnerability.

It can be difficult when someone is telling you you need to put on or lose at least 5 kilograms, you need to bulk up, slim down, you need to get bigger legs, smaller legs, a bigger bum, a smaller bum, bigger arms or smaller arms. This can lead to a lot of young athletes quitting because they don't want to change their body image or shape for their sport. I remember it being quite a tough thing to reconcile in my brain as a young female. My way of thinking about this was that my body had to become a tool for my sport, as a vessel that made me go faster. All of this training is being invested to make my body go faster. I saw my body as a fighting machine. If I have large glutes (bum), bulky quads, arms, shoulders and neck muscles, it's because I'm faster than anyone else and these muscles are going to win me a medal. I celebrated my physique and power and so should you in whatever form it takes. Remember: Muscles take a long time and a lot of hard work to grow. To maintain and keep them you have to constantly work hard in the gym and lift heavy. The day you stop sport, retire or move on, you will be able to slowly shed and get rid of the extra new unwanted muscles. They don't have to be there your whole life if you don't want them.

In my role as mentor for young skeleton competitors I've been asked questions by athletes in their early twenties saying they don't feel comfortable talking about their weight, how they struggle to put on sufficient weight as well as female athletes talking about their periods and adapting training around them. A female athlete's menstrual cycle can affect how they feel day to day, and therefore how they train. Struggling with period pains, experiencing bad cramps and hot flushes each month isn't fun. A female's monthly cycle of hormones has a powerful effect on the body's system, emotions and mood.

There is now a lot more awareness and some great resources out there to advise girls and their coaches on how to adapt training differently at different points of their cycle. During your period week while in the gym, having chatted with your coach, you might lift slightly lighter weights during your cycle. Oestrogen, the hormone that is increased during menstruation, can increase the elasticity of joints in the days before ovulation. This could lead to higher risk of injuries such as anterior cruciate ligament (ACL) problems, which occur if a knee or lower leg is twisted. Monitoring on apps and keeping a diary can be useful to pick up patterns and I'd suggest speaking to your coaches who can help point you in the right direction, giving you full and confidential advice should you need it. Take a look at the English Institute of Sport (EIS) that has launched the SmartHer campaign, which prioritises female health, dealing with topics from periods to urinary incontinence, and supports athletes during their careers.

Always be comfortable, never feel alone, and be open and confident in speaking about what's on your mind. How you feel does affect your performance, realising that this is completely normal, and that you can talk about it with your coaches or another female on the team is really important. It's a similar principle to working with your personality; a happy athlete is a better athlete.

LUCK

Another thing that you'll almost certainly encounter along the way is luck.

Luck can strike at any time and be a blessing or a curse. Every athlete of any age will experience good and bad luck, I've certainly had my share of both. Luck is about how you deal with it, what you learn from it and how you can make the most of it.

ELITE INSIGHT

Colin Jackson CBE –
1988 Seoul Olympic Silver Medallist, World, European and Commonwealth Champion, 110-Metre Hurdles:

The road will never be smooth, you will get injured, that's a given situation when working so hard, but don't fear it, you are not the first and 100% not the last to suffer, so keep positive, seek help and trust yourself. Talent doesn't disappear overnight, take the time needed to return, don't rush, coming back too quickly could be your downfall!

In many instances (sadly not all), you can create your own luck. To this day I consider myself lucky to have found a sport I had a real talent for and one that's given me so many incredible experiences.

But how much of this was luck?

I was first exposed to skeleton by spending time at a gym that was regularly used by bobsleigh and skeleton athletes. I remember watching Alex Coomber on TV at the Salt Lake City 2002 Winter Olympic Games winning a brilliant bronze medal. I consider myself fortunate to have met these people (and mustered the courage to invite myself along to their training), to have seen Alex bring the sport to the attention of the British audience and to live near the UK's only push track. But it isn't lost on me that I found myself in that situation because I was already a committed athlete who was always at the gym. Leading up this point, I'd still been training hard with my athletics club, and had also started training with the British Modern Pentathlon team based in Bath. I had an offer to join the lottery-funded GB talent squad. I enjoyed it and was starting to get good at it, but I learned the possibilities of representing Great Britain were greater in a different sport. The events that eventually led me to showing potential at that skeleton training camp in Lillehammer were undoubtedly filled with luck. But the promise I showed was fundamental in my future success. The reasons coaches saw potential in me was down to being in good physical condition from years of training in another sport. Luck presented me with the opportunity, and hard work had put me in a position to seize it.

Whichever sport you're currently in, give it everything you have, you just never know if another talent might reveal itself along the way. Create your own luck.

"TAKE EVERY OPPORTUNITY TO GIVE SOMETHING AGO. SAY YES. YOU HAVE NOTHING TO LOSE".

That said, sometimes luck is something you simply have no control over. In skeleton the obvious factor is the weather. There's a track in East Germany called Winterberg, where you can have every season of weather in the space of an hour. The start of the race might be blue sky and sunshine, then 15 minutes later it's gone from foggy and misty to heavy snow. You can experience every possible weather condition across the duration of one race so the sliding conditions will mean very good luck for some and very bad luck for others.

Similarly in St. Moritz, Switzerland, the only track where we all badly wanted a later start time. The temperature can reach anything between −15 and −25° degrees (bad enough for the athletes, but the poor coaches had to stand there for hours!). As the day goes on and the weather very slightly warms up, a thin layer of water forms on the track, helping the athletes have less contact with the ice and making them slide quicker due to the lower friction. Neither the competitors with the good luck or the bad luck could do anything about it.

You'll find yourself in situations like this throughout your sporting career where the deck of cards is well and truly stacked against you, no matter how much the event may mean to you.

REMIND YOURSELF

Never let situations take control of you. <u>Don't</u> get **FRUSTRATED, MAD or ANGRY** about it. It is the same for other athletes in the competition. You still **NEED To FOCUS** on the **POSITIVES** and deal with the situation as best you can. You still need to **PERFORM** to your **BEST ABILITY** even in less than ideal conditions.

ELITE INSIGHT

Heather Fell –
2008 Beijing Olympic Medallist, World and European
Champion; Modern Pentathlon

My journey between leaving school and standing on the podium
at the Olympics was far from smooth. The difficult and dark periods
throughout that journey certainly made winning that medal even
sweeter. See any challenges and obstacles in your path as opportunities to make you stronger, you'll be amazed at how far that strength
will then take you.

You may have a lot of pressure to achieve a good result for
ranking points or medals, but sometimes you just have to accept
the luck is against you and try not to get too frustrated or angry
to the point it affects your mental state for training and future
events. The reality is that sometimes conditions will work against
you. Allowing this to cause too much frustration will only hinder
you and distract your focus. Go with it, make the best of it and
remain focussed on constant improvement over blame and
frustration.

The same advice goes for any aspect of bad luck during any
sport. Imagine you're in a triathlon and there's a bike crash in front
of you that knocks you off or slows you down. Your options are
to complain and moan about your cursed luck or to keep your
focus on the rest of the race. You don't know what's still ahead of

you so grit it out and maintain the same mindset you had at the start of the race. Speed skating is a great example of this, we've seen many situations where the top three in a race crash near the finish line and the athletes further down the pack suddenly come through and win. They could have let themselves become frustrated or annoyed at their position and subconsciously eased off. Or they can give everything they have at all times and get their rewards.

Note to Self

"Never, Never, Never quit or give up. Always stay focused on the goal ahead".

Even stood standing at the top of a track knowing the conditions meant I had little chance of winning was a good lesson. I learned to take a deep breath, get on with it and make absolutely sure I was going to make the best of myself and the conditions I'd been given. I didn't realise it at the time, but I was learning how to control my emotions. I was training myself physically and tactically to perform in bad conditions. I was building greater resilience to the point where adversity becomes less of a hindrance to my mindset in the future. Most importantly, I was learning to *control the controllables*.

DISTRACTIONS

With all this being said, there's something else that's an inevitable part of being a teenager, distractions!

ELITE INSIGHT

Susie Rodgers MBE –
2012 London Paralympic ×3 Bronze Medallist, 2016 Rio de Janeiro Paralympic Gold and ×2 Bronze, Multiple World Championship Medallist; Swimming:

I started my journey into elite sport quite late. When I was at school, the PE teachers didn't really know what to do with me when it came to sport lessons, because of my disability. So, I was frequently left in the library if it was deemed the exercise might be difficult for me or I couldn't take part. I did do some sport, like swimming, but I didn't get any encouragement and the Paralympics were not as visible as they are today, so I naturally focused on my studies and other career options. At university, I did "dip my toe" into swimming, competing nationally, but again, that mindset of sport not being a viable career for me propelled me towards graduating and then embarking on a career outside of sport. It was only when I settled in London with a full-time job that I started to develop my career as an athlete, picking up from where I left off at university. I was training around my working week of

35+ hours in the office in my 20s. I remember running out of the office at 4pm to catch the train from London Bridge to Crystal Palace, training 2 hours then catching the train back to my flat in central London, getting in after 10.30 pm. I would get up and do the whole thing again the next day! I remember doing fewer sessions at the start to accommodate my schedule, but I made sure that they were quality sessions with my coach. I also had to consume more calories because I quickly realised that commuting and running all over London, plus training, especially with one arm and one leg, was definitely going to take it out of me! The bonus of commuting was that it made me super, super fit. I started to realise that what I did around my swimming was actually part of my training. I was getting cardio by walking or sometimes running to catch my train. This was a big learning curve. My nutritionist at the time followed me for a day to get an idea of what I was doing and quickly picked up on the fact that I wasn't fuelling myself properly. I went into London 2012 still working part-time and went straight back to my work. A few years later, I did go on sabbatical before Rio 2016 and perhaps that is why I had more success there, because I focused completely on my swimming. However, it was detrimental to my mental health – I need to work and use my brain, sport just isn't enough for me. In fact, on sabbatical, I was attending voluntary board meetings and continuing to learn throughout. Looking back, I am not sure if the sabbatical from work was the key to my success but rather, with time, a more focused and mature approach to my swimming and a better understanding of the sport I was in. I would say that it is individual. Some athletes are comfortable with putting everything into their sport, but personally, I think it is damaging to put all your eggs in one basket. It heaps a huge amount of pressure on you to do well. You cope better with losses, injury, illness and failure, potentially, if you have other things that you can invest your energy in as well. So, my advice is to think about your future beyond your sport. It will end and not everyone can or will want to go into the media and commentating circles. Keep up your learning, education is power, make sure you think deeply beyond your identity as an athlete about the things that motivate you personally and professionally and invest time in those things as well. Yes, do give 100% to your sport in training and preparation, but equally you do have room to give some energy to developing yourself as well. There is time in between sessions, rest time and recovery, there is always time, but you need to manage that time and be efficient with it. I don't regret one bit keeping my career going, even if it may have been frowned upon in sporting circles, because it is my future and only I can invest in that – no one else.

Distractions will happen, especially if you're a teenager. There may be moments in your life when other things come along and push sports down your priority list. I don't think you should pressurize and push yourself too much if it's not the right time to do so. I only got into skeleton when I was 18. I was probably around 14 when I really started to love athletics and take it seriously. I loved the training, loved having different friendships, going to the club, getting better and better, seeing that stopwatch showing faster and faster times. Even then, my parents didn't force me if I didn't want to go. They knew that if my athletic success was going to be long term and sustainable then it needed to come from the passion within me, not by my doing something I didn't want to. Eventually this happened and I'm so pleased that I was given the space and time to find that passion. I loved sports, so I kept doing it.

If you find yourself becoming distracted from training in your teen years, don't beat yourself up about it. The passion will come back if it's the right thing for you. You have time on your side.

Training and competing will be far more effective if it's something you actively want to do.

Of course, moving from good to great will eventually require a big commitment to training, but don't see distractions as a barrier to this. Live your life, if the higher levels of sport are the right direction for you, you'll know. When you've figured this out, go for it with everything you have.

ATHLETE IN FOCUS

Jason Gardener MBE,
2004 Athens 4 × 100-Metre Relay Olympic Champion, Multiple World Indoor Champion, European Indoor Champion, Multiple Commonwealth Champion, 100-Metre and 60-Metre Sprint

I have had to overcome barriers my whole life to make it to the top of the podium winning Olympic, World, Commonwealth and European Championship titles. Every barrier was an important learning experience to overcome and whilst sometimes soul-destroying they certainly enabled me to become resilient and develop my mental toughness to achieve high level performances. At times I felt like my life was ending with the failures at critical times, but now I look back and can see how important they were as part of the journey. Hindsight can be a wonderful thing.

Before the days of Lottery Funding and the World Class Performance System, I grew up with no proper athletic facilities in Bath and we adapted to make the most out of the facilities and environments we were operating in. My coach and I would always use the lack of high-quality facilities and support services as a focus to be smarter with our training and use this as a motivation to beat my rivals who had more privileged circumstances.

In terms of thinking outside the box, I remember we used Vauxhall car wheels and tires inflated to go onto an Olympic bar enabling us to drop the weights without breaking the floor in the school gym and more importantly without damaging my back during the power cleans and snatch lifting sessions. We couldn't afford the expensive rubber Olympic weights at the time and this provided a good solution.

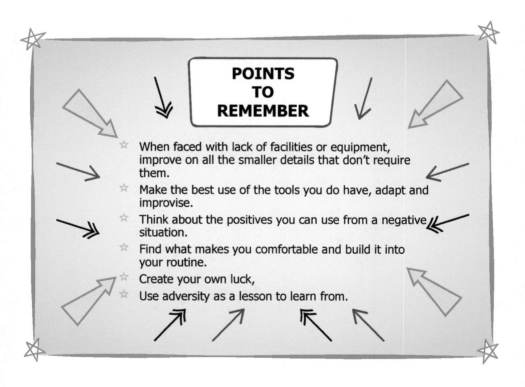

POINTS TO REMEMBER

☆ When faced with lack of facilities or equipment, improve on all the smaller details that don't require them.

☆ Make the best use of the tools you do have, adapt and improvise.

☆ Think about the positives you can use from a negative situation.

☆ Find what makes you comfortable and build it into your routine.

☆ Create your own luck,

☆ Use adversity as a lesson to learn from.

3 Managing Setbacks, Injury and Fear

Think of a sportsperson you admire from any era and any sport. Then think of the images that appear in your mind when you do so. It might be Sally Gunnell holding aloft the Union Jack flag after winning the Olympics (as it is for me, when I do this exercise); it might be Wayne Rooney scoring an overhead kick, Venus Williams or Andy Murray leaping for joy at Wimbledon, Lewis Hamilton punching the air after winning another F1 race, or Jessica Ennis-Hill powering down the finishing straight to win gold in 2012. These moments of triumph are powerful, inspiring, joyous and unforgettable. We don't often think about the journey that these athletes went through to reach these points in their life. Every one of them (and every athlete that's ever taken part in any sport) has experienced setbacks of varying degrees. Whatever your motivation for sports and how high you want to go, there'll be setbacks along the way. You might get injured, you might face fear and you might face failure. If any or all of these (or more besides) happen to you, it's how you respond to them that'll determine your ability to bounce back and that's what this chapter aims to help you with.

INJURIES AND INJURY PREVENTION

The setback that everyone in every sport at every level has suffered is the dreaded injuries. The human body is amazing, but occasionally (or regularly, for some), it's going to let us down. I was in a sport that risked not only the typical sprinter's injury, but also the addition of being in that awkward bent over running position, not to mention high speed and walls! If I wanted to be successful in skeleton it was essential that I did everything I could to both prevent injuries and bounce back from them when they happened.

ELITE INSIGHT

Colin Jackson CBE –
1988 Seoul Olympic Silver Medallist, World, European and Commonwealth Champion, 110-Metre Hurdles

The road will never be smooth, you will get injured, that's a given situation when working so hard, but don't fear it. You are not the first and 100% not the last to suffer, so keep positive, seek help, and trust yourself, talent doesn't disappear overnight, take the time needed to return, don't rush. Coming back too quickly could be your downfall.

My first injury was a pretty horrible crash on an infamous track called Altenberg in Germany that we used to call Alten-smash. Let's just say the local hospital airlifting service was busy there. I basically got spat out of a corner, my sled was at the wrong angle, I was inexperienced, I didn't know what to do to correct my sled and then smash, I hit the wall hard, my body twisted awkwardly and just like that, I was experiencing my first dose of injury (and fear).

My instant reaction was that I was ready to stop skeleton altogether. I felt horrendous, I was scared stiff. I remember one of my teammates hugged me afterwards and was genuinely shocked that I didn't quit the sport afterwards. I think he always saw me as this little, shy, sensitive girl that would have quit the sport. But I had something inside me that said no, I'm not going to let that corner get me again. I have to beat it. That said, it wasn't' an immediate reaction. While I couldn't go straight back down, due to a slight concussion and a broken sled, I was still well aware that after crashing, I just had to get back on this track as soon as I possibly could. This is also where I benefitted from some tough loving coaches. They weren't overly dramatic, they encouraged me to study video, find out where I went wrong, then go back down the track with a new focus. They taught me to think logically rather than emotionally, which you'll read more about later in the book.

Without knowing it at the time, this crash slipped (my first) disc in my back. Shortly after, when I was back in the UK and looking after some horses that lived near me, I remember a horse rubbing its bridle on my back after a ride, and then going to watch Bath rugby play. It was freezing cold and I stood up after sitting for a while and I just couldn't move. My whole back locked up, seized up. After some medical examinations and scans, I was told it was a slipped disc. That initial crash at Altenberg had given me my first skeleton injury – I was lucky to get away with only a bad back.

The silver lining to this injury was the lessons it taught me about the importance of doing all the right preparation. I became obsessive with following the instructions the physios gave me, the stability exercises, the rehab exercises. I followed them to the letter, I made sure my commitment was full and continuous in order to protect that injury, help with recovery and avoid future ones. Every morning I would get out of bed, lay on the floor and do 5–10 minutes of simple exercises, then later at the gym another 20–30 minutes of specific rehab exercise. As a personal trainer now, I often work with clients who are recovering from injuries, and it's so common for people to get frustrated at the length of time they're taking to recover.

"Have you been doing all of your rehab exercise?" I'd ask. Unless the answer is a firm "yes", then the reasons for the longer than expected rehabilitation process are easily explained!

Whenever you're injured, follow your rehab program with as much commitment as you do your training. Rehab will not only help you overcome injuries, it'll also help to prevent future ones. Don't cut corners.

The back injury taught me the seriousness of warming up, of activating the muscles, of doing all of those drills with relentless dedication. It was drilled into me because I never wanted to get the sort of injuries that are preventable.

Always wear warm clothes, get your muscles as warm as you possibly can so you minimise the risk of injury. Look at examples like professional rugby teams. The substitutes aren't on the sideline in their shorts and t-shirts anymore, they're in thick, warm gear, they're warming up on exercise bikes, because sports have realised how important it is to keep those muscles really warm. It's sometimes inevitable in rugby that you can get injured from a hit or an awkward tackle, your job as an athlete in any sport is to prevent those injuries that are preventable. As well as reducing the risk of injury, your performance is increased too. Even if it's a warm day outside, still wear warm clothes, keep your tracksuit on. Still make sure you're really warm to protect your muscles.

I used to carry around a hot water bottle with me all the time. I even had a small travel kettle because some of the places we stayed didn't have a kettle. I'd shove the mini hot water bottle down the back of my salopettes so it was constantly keeping my back warm in those cold temperatures. If there was any way I could find to be constantly warm before and during a competition (and training), then I was going to find it and use it.

Injury maintenance should be a constant part of your routine, don't wait until you've had an injury before you learn a harsh lesson. Some can't be prevented; there are freak accidents that can happen and sometimes your body can just break down, but you maximise your chances of avoiding them by being equally disciplined with your stretching, warming up and learning safe and proper exercise techniques.

Learning is a key aspect for all athletes (hopefully you've made a good start by reading this book). Take personal responsibility to educate yourself in all aspects of training, preparation and recovery.

I realise now that most of us can have a part of our body that is out of alignment in some areas and yet we train at 100% day in and day out without looking into what would be the safest and most efficient ways to exercise. Read, watch YouTube, find every *credible* source you can and give yourself the best chance to remain as injury-free as you can.

The physios used to tell me it was like rust on a chain, once you've had one injury, more follow if you keep training hard. The more injuries you prevent through educating yourself, the less you'll have throughout your career and beyond.

For years I had crunching painful knees that were catching and grinding. So while I was still a competing athlete, at the end of my winter season I had to undergo two knee operations on both knees on two different occasions. This was initially down to wear and tear and taking some pretty hard knocks on some of the tracks. I had my meniscus removed, bits of broken cartilage cleaned up and taken out and my knee caps smoothed off as they were horrible and spiky underneath.

Since retiring I have undergone a further two major knee operations, one from a big accident in the gym ironically the week I said I was retiring! This snapped most of the ligaments all around my knee and required major surgery and months and months of rehab. The last operation was knee alignment surgery, which I needed as my kneecap was falling to one side – to put it simply. So, now I have some amazing big scars over and around both knees and several bolts added! Both required a massive amount of hard work and pure focus and dedication to the rehab exercises that needed to be done several times a day for many months.

I also have many degenerative and some bulging discs in my back and neck from that first crash I had in Altenberg, Germany, and from a bad crash I had on the push track in Bath. I had to undergo loads of work to keep my back as pain-free as possible, even though it's never been pain-free and isn't to this day.

I list these injuries as a way of highlighting that despite all of the work I did to prevent them, they still happened. I actually consider myself to have a pretty good record with staying healthy. I'm proud to say that for example I've never pulled a hamstring, calf or quadricep muscle during a sprint session because I always prepared my body as best as I could. I spent extra time in the gym doing stability exercises before and after every session.

I always came out of every injury physically and mentally stronger than I was before. You can still focus and work on all other areas of your sport even though you may not be able to do the physical side. Look through that pie chart that I talked about in chapter 5. Where are other areas of your life that need improvement?

Can you look at the technical side of your sport and get to know your equipment better? Can you start to research tactics or other teams' performances, to better your own?

Can you improve your diet and nutrition, make better food choices, start preparing meals?

There is always something you can do to become stronger and perform better even if you are nursing an injury. You will have highs and lows with injuries, but you can come out of an injury physically and mentally stronger.

Fight through it, be dedicated, stay positive and do everything you can to minimise risk.

ELITE INSIGHT

Maria Costello MBE –
Motorcycle Racer, Former World Record Holder, First Female Podium Finisher, Manx Grand Prix 2005

My sport and particularly the Isle of Man TT races are seen as some of most dangerous motorcycle races in the world.

Despite the danger, fear and tremendous mental and physical challenges surrounding this event, plus the fact that I compete on equal terms with the guys (something that I also cherish) this is the race that I take the most pleasure in.

It's the one that has given me my greatest achievements amongst and alongside my heroes and legends of this sport. TT Female lap record, Guinness World Record, first woman to stand on the podium in a race around the TT course, multiple podiums at the Manx Grand Prix (its sister event), making history by becoming one of few and the only woman to have raced a sidecar and solo motorcycle at the TT and my absolute highlight of a podium finish at the Classic TT alongside 23 times TT winner John McGuinness.

I'm not blind to the danger, I have experienced the pain of 24 broken bones during my career and the worst crash of my career happened at the Isle of Man.

My desire, drive and determination to continue to succeed at what's seen as the toughest challenge for man and machine outweighs all the pain and sacrifice.

It's true that you can't actually remember pain and once the physical pain of broken bones and operations that often follow has left the body, my want to race floods back almost stronger than before.

Despite all the heartache, all those glimpses of hope are still very much worthwhile. I kept my thoughts focussed on the big-end goal and what I knew I could still achieve in the sport. If I get this corner right, and shave a second off my time, then I can get a top ten finish, this was always in the back of my mind, despite the low points and occasionally broken body.

ATHLETE IN FOCUS

Vanessa Ruck –
"The Girl on a Bike", Motorbike Racer, Adventurer,
Social Curator

I was all about extreme sports. My whole lifestyle was adrenaline sports, pushing my body and mind to the limits. Kite surfing was my main activity, if there was no wind we'd wakeboard, mountain bike, rock climb, snowboarding. I was at the gym every day, I cycled to work for sixteen miles every day. I was incredibly fit. March 2014 all of this changed, all of this as taken away. For the next seven years it's been a roller coaster. Everything has been aimed at having a pain-free body, I don't currently have a pain-free body, but I have one that I can make do with because it's the only one I'll ever have. I'm not going to stop doing the pushing it & doing the sports that I want to because of the enjoyment and the pleasure I get out of them.

I have a reconstructed shoulder and right hip, I've had seven surgeries. There's an element of the recovery where some people, or I, even thought that as I'd had them before, they'd be much easier as I knew what was coming. It actually felt like it got harder. The scar tissue took longer to heal & I found myself going back down to what felt like rock bottom again, as far as that mental journey goes.

I visualised recovery for me like being in a tunnel, so you're in this tunnel & right at the end is a bit of light. I was concentrating on my recovery, I was doing my physio, I was eating well, I was looking after my body, I was following medical advice & slowly getting closer & closer to that light. I saw myself slowly making some gains, my physio was slowly upping my activity & that light was getting brighter and brighter & I thought I was so close to the end of my recovery. But in my journey, I just kept hitting a ceiling, where the balance of the pain and the novelty of being able to get back to my activities was forefront in my mind. Medical guys were telling me I could gradually start to do more, but I knew that my body was still in a lot of pain. I knew my body and it wasn't right, so I'd tell the doctors that it wasn't right, so they'd check again & see that they missed something. Just like that, the tunnel would feel like a mile longer, often with very little light at the end. I was in a never-ending road of pain and surgery and a broken body that couldn't do anything that I wanted it to.

Thankfully I realised that it's okay to not be okay.

Thankfully I had help and realised that me is me and I learned to accept me. Self-loathing and disappointment doesn't make you stronger. Focussing on goals and setting goals and doing things that can make you smile each day do make you stronger.

The important part of my goal setting was making sure they were realistic, so I could manage my expectations. Initially I'd set myself too high expectations in my early goals and I've learnt to get better at this. Initially I was so hopeful to hit certain expectations, but the reality was that there was no way my body would be ready. But with the best will in the world, it doesn't physically repair you.

So my goals became manageable in terms of my expectation. They were simple things like not weeing myself in bed, being able to go to the bathroom on my own, being able to put my own socks on. My husband became so good at plaiting my hair because for so long there was no way I'd have been able to have done that.

I learnt that little things each day would turn into big milestones. Going downstairs to eat dinner, making it out to the garden would really lift my spirits. Sometimes just a change of scenery would be incredibly uplifting, so I'd switch from a "day bed" to a "night bed" which felt like a big achievement.

Then I'd set stretch goals, goals that were going to keep me going, beyond what I was capable of today, tomorrow or next week. So my first stretch goal was deciding I wanted to get an off road dirt-bike.

It was five months before I could even sit on it, but I had it, it was there and it was a goal. Every time I felt like I hurt too much or I couldn't find the energy or I just didn't want to do my physio, that bike was sat there saying "come on, we need to go for a ride".

So for me it was that mix of short-term and long-term goal setting that were realistic.

When you set recovery goals that you simply can't achieve, emotionally it becomes really hard.

A big goal for me is one day going back to kite surfing. Emotionally this will be incredibly difficult because I can compare my pre-accident capabilities to what they are now. This is easier with bike riding now, because I have no comparison, I didn't do it prior to the accident and at the moment I'm not willing to take that emotional risk, so it's very much a stretch goal.

My advice to anyone who has suffered, or is currently suffering an injury that's taken you away from doing something you love is, first, that it's okay to feel low. If you're hurting or you're in a bad place, don't beat yourself up for not feeling okay. Doing this is just like beating a bruise, if you're not okay, then you're not okay. Take steps that are in your control, find things that will put a smile on your face. For me, as little as this may seem, it was mango! Clearly this isn't a major thing, but it was just a little bit of happiness. If you can find a few things (they don't even have to include mango!) like that, that you can put into your day to lift your spirits. I'd advise you to remember and recognise that pain changes your attitude, so if you're grumpy to a checkout person at a supermarket, they're most likely going to be grumpy back at you. Be aware of what you're projecting. I worked hard at having conscious awareness of what energies I was putting out, because that's usually the energies that come back to you.

Then start to think about what powers you do have in your control. It's very easy to say, "It's not fair, I'm going to hide under my duvet, the world's against me". But then I thought about the battles that so many people are fighting, many of which can't be seen and many of which are far worse than those that I'm fighting. I couldn't change things by feeling sorry for myself, so what powers do I have that are in my control? Well, for one thing I could be absolutely committed to my physio. I hear from many people who may talk of having a bad back, so I ask them if they're doing their physio? More often than not they aren't and therefore shouldn't really complain.

The next part to this is your nutrition. Your body is what you eat. If you fill yourself with processed food then you won't have the energy or the healing capabilities to conquer what you're battling.

The final part of injury recovery is to not rush it. When you think about the grand scheme of life (which is difficult when you're a teenager), then an extra week or month to let an injury really settle and really heal is so much more beneficial than rushing back too quickly and causing long-term damage. Be fair to your body as far as the recovery timelines go. Remember the long-term gains over the short-term ones.

To this point, I've spoken about recovery and rehabilitation of injuries. The more serious end of this is when an injury can take away your sport altogether, as happened to me. I can tell you that this is brutally hard. It may be a cliché, but I had to learn that one door closes and another opens, albeit it can and will take a long time to realise this. Take a step back and think about what tools you have. Which skills are still in your control? How can you shift and realign and take it to something in parallel to what you were able to do previously? You'll find that there are a lot of transferable things that you can apply in this situation.

Kite surfing was my main activity and to have this taken away was pretty horrific, I also have to accept that I'll never be able to run again. But there are many other things I can do with my time. I learnt to think that running isn't the be all and end all of life. I can still ride a bike and there are people with worse injuries than me. For me it's a case of counting the blessings I do still have, for one thing, I could very easily have died. It took a serious amount of mental headspace to take a step back and think that even in the situation I'm in now, I'm lucky.

Injuries, whether serious or minor, can sometimes be the catalyst for even greater things. For me, *The Girl on a Bike* wouldn't exist if I hadn't been hit by that car. Sharing the battles that I was going through was something that resonated with a lot of people as well as giving me the opportunity to connect with the world to some extent. If anyone had told me seven years ago that I'd ride motorbikes and connect with so many people on social media I'd have probably choked on my drink. I've learnt to relentlessly look for the positives in every possible situation.

FEAR

Fear comes in many forms for those competing in sports and is yet another possible setback that can negatively affect the performance of an athlete. There's the obvious physical fear if you're about to be tackled by a hulking rugby player, you're heading into a boxing match or yes about to hurtle down an ice track face first at 90 mph. There's also fear of not making a team, letting people down, letting yourself down, fear of equipment that you don't know or trust, fear of injuries and wrapping yourself in cotton wool, fear of drugs or what goes into your body so you don't leave your water bottle unattended, fear of other teammates or competitors, of not getting the results you need for positions or lottery funding, fear of pressure and expectations, fear of failure and many more besides.

This list sounds a little daunting, but that isn't the intention. The intention is to show that all athletes will experience one or more of these at some stage in their sports journeys. You aren't alone in feeling fear; it's an entirely natural process that like many other setbacks can be responded to and turned into positive energy.

ELITE INSIGHT

Freddie Burns –
Gloucester, Leicester, Bath, England, Rugby Union

In rugby you're fortunate that the games keep coming. If you win, it's an immediate chance to kick on, if you lose, an immediate opportunity to bounce straight back.

The difficulty is controlling your emotions from week to week and not letting them get the better of you either with the complacency of over-confidence after a win, or the disheartening blow of failure after a loss.

It wasn't till I was 7 years into my playing career that a coach said a phrase that I still use to this day. "You're never as good as you think you

were but you're never as bad you think you were". A very simple statement but one that opened my eyes and allowed me to always take a
balanced view on match day events and push forward in my career
whilst minimising the extreme ups and downs that sport serves up on
a weekly basis.

I'm often asked if competing in skeleton meant that I was fearless.
The short answer is no, absolutely not. I think skeleton athletes
or athletes in any kind of high-risk sport experience fear just like
anyone else, we just learn to control it and work with it. You can
too, in whatever sport you're in.

I experienced so many different kinds of fears throughout my
career. I remember being at the World Championships in 2009 in
Lake Placid, needing the best result of my life, with a top three
position to secure lottery funding and Olympic qualification.
As (bad) luck would have it, I was ill in the lead-up to the
competition. I'd missed a lot of training, felt truly awful and was
throwing up the night before. Everything I'd been aiming for was
now under very serious threat and the fear of failure was almost
unbearable. I had to make a conscious decision to either let the
fear take hold and stew on my misfortune, or say to myself "you
know what Amy, just slide". Thankfully I made the correct mental
decision and won a silver medal. Your mind is an incredibly
powerful tool, use it positively. You can feel bad about your
emotions but you need to be in control of them.

The fear of failure is constant and it reflects reality, there are no
guarantees you will achieve your potential. Just because you
want to win it doesn't mean you will. You need to take positive
and practical steps, both physically and mentally, to overcome
your fears.

During summer training, we had physical tests every 2 months, sprint tests, strength tests, swot analyses, everything. We always needed to perform, to hit our specific sprint times, explosive jump heights, sled pull sprint times and weight lifting targets. If you weren't reaching them, at any point you could be kicked off the team. We always had to be improving, always had to be performing. We needed to show our strength output was improving and our speed and power were improving. These were the times when for me, fear was used as a motivation. Am I okay skipping a training session? What if I slack off the healthy eating for a little while, will it be fine eventually? No, the fear of dropping out of the team led to more determination, more drive, more focus, more motivation because I knew if I didn't perform, there are plenty others who want to take my place.

I used many different techniques to help me overcome my fear. Those that proved the most effective for me were making a conscious decision to challenge my own thought processes if I felt they were holding me back and beating them down with positive affirmations. Here are two examples:

Negative question: "Why am I so slow?"

Positive affirmation: "I am not as fast as I'd like to be right now, but, I am going to focus on: driving my knees through, my breathing, my preparation".

Negative question: "Why are the other girls going faster than me?"

Positive affirmation: "Is it helpful in the here and now that I judge myself based on how the other girls run? My ability is totally independent of how someone else is performing, work on myself".

TURNING −ve to a +ve

NEGATIVE

POSITIVE

✘ <u>Don't</u>

✓ <u>Do</u>

EXAMPLE:
"I feel terrible and slow today"

- _____

- _____

- _____

- _____

- _____

- _____

- _____

- _____

- _____

EXAMPLE:
"I will concentrate on my technique"

- _____

- _____

- _____

- _____

- _____

- _____

- _____

- _____

- _____

Make sure you put a lot of emphasis on whether your thinking is helping you to focus and achieve your goals. Don't underestimate the power of your thought processes and how subtle changes to them can make you a far better and far less fearful athlete.

ELITE INSIGHT

Hannah White –
World Record Holder, Sailor, Broadcaster, Adventurer

I was in the middle of the Atlantic in a boat by myself and I had to go to the top of the mast to repair something. The mast is around fifty feet high, the boat moves twenty degrees side to side on the water, making the mast move sixty degrees, I was crashing against the mast while climbing it, it was horrific. When I reached the top I'd realised that I hadn't organised my kit properly and I had no way of climbing safely back down. The only way I had of coming back down, was by untying myself and free climbing fifty feet to the bottom. I remember swinging back and forth at the top of the mast, crying. I then had the very clear thought that crying up here wasn't going to help me get back down. I could stay here crying for three days and no one is going to come and help so I may as well make the best of the situation (by climbing down!). This incident created a real shift in my attitude towards my sailing. I realised that in such extreme circumstances there was no room for emotion, no room to worry about things I couldn't control, I just had to get on and do the job that I needed to do. There's definitely a time for emotion, but you have to know when it's appropriate. At the top of the mast there was no time for it, that came later. If you're at the start of a 100-metre race or you're about to take a penalty in a penalty shootout, you need total focus and clarity, you can't be emotional, you need to channel it, park it until later and use it productively.

"DON'T LET YOUR **EMOTIONS** STOP YOU FROM DOING WHAT **NEEDS** TO BE **DONE**".

FAILURE

Now there's *fear* of failure and then there's just plain old *failure.* You think Sir Chris Hoy won every bike race he ever entered? Did Dame Kelly Holmes win every championship she ever took part in prior to winning double gold in Athens? Of course they didn't, but what they did do was learn from what they might have thought of as "failures" at the time, whether that be a bad performance on a given day, or an injury or anything else. They took those low moments and they stored them as fuel.

I certainly had a big failure in my career and you know what, it was the single most important thing that ever happened to me in my career.

ELITE INSIGHT

Jason Gardener MBE,
2004 Athens 4 x 100-Metre Relay Olympic Champion, Multiple World Indoor Champion, European Indoor Champion, Multiple Commonwealth Champion, 100-Metre and 60-Metre Sprint

Fear of failure was a vital ingredient to my success and continues to drive me. I use it to bring the best out of myself, when I am passionate and motivated about something and know how important an ingredient it is.

It was 2006 and I had dreams to go to the Turin Winter Olympics. I didn't make it. I wasn't going to be part of the team, I wasn't going to wear the GB vest, I wasn't going to be an Olympian. I'd failed myself.

I knew as soon as the competition season was finished I wasn't in the right ranking spot to make the team, I was told I was going to be a reserve. Even though I knew, there was still a gut feeling of intense frustration, I was so disappointed in myself. I could come up with all sorts of excuses, throw my toys out the pram and generally mope in self-pity, but once the reality set in, I had to turn it around. Once again, it was time to think logically rather than emotionally.

Yes, it feels rubbish, yes I'm heartbroken. Okay Amy, what are you going to do about it?

I was asked to go and be a commentator for BBC Five Live Radio at the games. Thinking emotionally about it would have meant ignoring it, refusing to watch, sulking and pretending like it wasn't even happening, refusing to go and do radio work for it.

Thinking logically, was there an opportunity to take a positive out of those 2006 games by going there? I'd never been to a Games before, I was still the official Skeleton Team reserve, but I used the commentating offer as a way to experience the atmosphere, to learn what it's like to be around an Olympic environment. It was incredible, I'd never experienced anything like it. Physically watching the race and seeing it happen was utterly invaluable. Seeing GB win a medal, soaking up everything I possibly could, talking to people, getting used to the mayhem and crazy mad atmosphere. It gave me so much drive and motivation to make *damn sure* I'd be there for the next one, in 2010. I made a promise to myself that day to make sure my feet would be on the start line, at the top of the track in Vancouver 2010, 4 years to that date I would be there.

The lessons from failure will be some of the most valuable you'll ever experience. See them for exactly that. Switch negative situations into fantastic learning experiences and get the best out of adversity.

Michael Jordan famously said, "I've missed more than 9000 shots in my career. I've lost almost 300 games. 26 times, I've been trusted to take the game winning shot and missed. I've failed over and over and over again in my life. And that is why I succeed".

REMIND YOURSELF

⭐ **IGNORE** others, don't focus on their performance.

⭐ Only put energy into what **YOU CAN CHANGE**.

⭐ Think **LOGICALLY** not emotionally.

⭐ Remain **FOCUSED** on your performance.

⭐ Don't worry about the "IF's".

⭐ Don't be nervous - you're "ENERGISED".

PERSEVERANCE

Setbacks aren't a "once every now and then" kind of thing. They'll keep appearing at varying levels of severity throughout your sporting life. Does it matter how many failures you've had? No. Does it matter if you keep having to fight through adversity? No. Does it matter that you still haven't achieved what you've set your heart on? No. Does it matter that no matter what you try, it doesn't seem to be working? No.

Do you know how many races I won in my 10-year career before I achieved my lifelong dream of Olympic gold?

None.

Persevere.

ATHLETE IN FOCUS

Jason Fox –
Former Special Forces Soldier, Television Presenter, Mental Health Advocate, Podcast Host

I know that I've had this conversation with myself, when I think "if I don't do it this time, I'm jacking it in". Midway through selection, when I was in the second phase I got badly injured, picked up a sickness & was flown out of the jungle. I'd failed. I remember lying in hospital for five days, the first two of which I was despondent at the thought of not being able to make it through selection. But on the third day I thought hang on a minute, this isn't over. Just because I had to go back to the beginning of selection due to trashing myself, that end vision of success was still there and if that's still here, then I'm still here. It was this mental focus on visualisation that gave me the kick up the backside that I needed. I wanted it that badly that I never gave up on it. Ultimately it's about that want, that desire & my genuine belief that I could do it.

Adding to this, I'm glad that I failed along the way. I feel like a better, more rounded person because I understand failure.

You've been going through four days of hell here & you probably find yourself questioning what is ultimately going to be thirty two weeks of the same. If you really want this, visualise yourself at the end, being presented with whatever achievement you've succeeded in. Then treat every day separately. See every day like a punch, deal with that one punch, don't have too much of a rigid long-term plan, be flexible in your mindset, embrace failure because it's the only thing that's going to make you better.

The most important thing I was ever taught was the phrase "cheer-fulness in the face of adversity". This isn't just about having a laugh (although that's important too), if you look into it a little deeper it means that no matter what happens, you've got to find the silver lining to every dark cloud. A positive mindset, even when everything feels like it's going wrong, is the only thing that's getting you through. If a rugby team is going through a bad run of form, if you can't laugh about it, you have no chance. You need to find that mindset inside to dig yourself out of whatever hole you find yourself in. The moment your head goes down and you think "I'm not doing it" then you're not doing it, it's not happening.

We need to see setbacks not as the "baddy" but as the "goody".

Setbacks can in hindsight be fantastic events sent to teach you certain lessons. Making any kind of the mistake is going to happen. Some mistakes will be small, some will be very big.

You're going to learn from every single one of them. It's a vital part of improving. As long as you keep learning how to use those experiences to make you a better athlete and to make you more prepared for the next challenge that you may have, you'll see setbacks in the way they should be seen.

Always take time to think about why something went wrong, why an injury happened, why you didn't succeed in a competition like you thought you would. Write these things down and make it a learning exercise.

Don't let any setbacks ever stop you from pursuing your ultimate dream. Take control of it, don't ever let it overwhelm you. You're in charge of the setbacks, they aren't in charge of you.

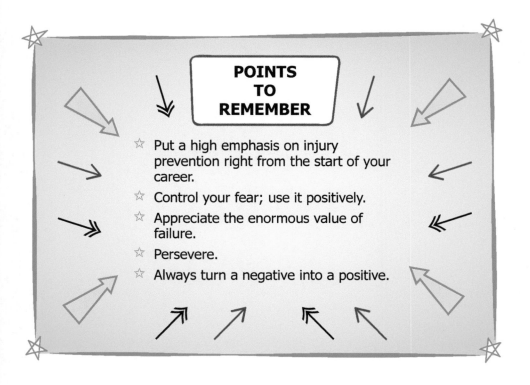

POINTS TO REMEMBER

☆ Put a high emphasis on injury prevention right from the start of your career.

☆ Control your fear; use it positively.

☆ Appreciate the enormous value of failure.

☆ Persevere.

☆ Always turn a negative into a positive.

4 Teamwork

Whether you're an individual athlete like I was or you're in a team sport, your success or failure will be significantly impacted by how effectively you use teamwork.

This chapter is all about the different ways you can get the most out of those around you (and help them get the best out of themselves). We'll discuss areas like trust, accountability, support networks, teammates, wider teams and conflict resolution.

Our philosophy within the British Skeleton Team was that the athlete was in the middle and those wider layers of team members around them were there to help them to do their very best.

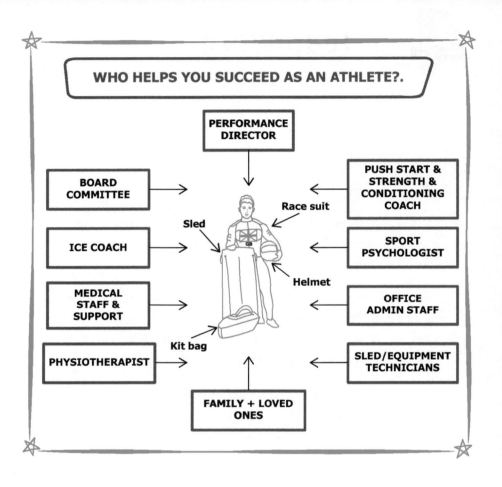

WHO HELPS YOU SUCCEED AS AN ATHLETE?.

PERFORMANCE DIRECTOR

BOARD COMMITTEE

PUSH START & STRENGTH & CONDITIONING COACH

Race suit

Sled

ICE COACH

SPORT PSYCHOLOGIST

Helmet

MEDICAL STAFF & SUPPORT

OFFICE ADMIN STAFF

Kit bag

PHYSIOTHERAPIST

SLED/EQUIPMENT TECHNICIANS

FAMILY + LOVED ONES

The team for me as an individual athlete was my strength coach in the gym, my ice coach, my physio (especially if you're like me and spent an awful lot of time on the physio bed), and there were the powers that be above – the committee members, the support staff, the performance director. There were my direct teammates within Team GB and my competitors from across the world. Then there's the whole next level of support with family and friends.

If you want to get the best out of yourself and reach the elite levels of competition, then this wide variety of people can help you in many different ways. One thing is for sure, I didn't win my gold medal on my own.

TRUST

"THE **BEST** HIGH **PERFORMING TEAMS** ARE BUILT ON **TRUST**, THIS GIVES YOU **SUCCESS**".

Let's begin by looking at the area that I've always felt is the single most important in a team environment: trust. This goes for you and your ability to trust your team, as well as you demonstrating that you're a trusted member of the team.

If I was going to hurtle down an ice track face first at 90 mph and chase a lifelong Olympic dream, then I was going to feel a lot more confident about doing so if I had full faith in the team helping me to do it. At the Olympics, having the ability to solely concentrate on my race was invaluable and this would have been so much more difficult if I had other things to worry about. I was lucky to have Rachel Blackburn there as our sled technician and co-designer of the sled I raced on. She did the service the evening before my race, checking it thoroughly, making sure all the bolts, nuts and screws were okay in the inner frames – a little bit like a car getting a mot or service. This was something I'd normally have to do myself as an athlete and can take several hours. You can imagine the level of trust that you'd need to have in someone to do this check for you. My belief in Rachel, based on a long time of seeing her doing her job to such a high standard, is a nice example of how valuable this belief in another person can be. I would then make sure the taping was correct, making sure there were no holes that could affect aerodynamics and checking that the metal runners were as scratch free as they could be, polishing them up with special paper.

ELITE INSIGHT

Rebecca Adlington OBE –
Olympic, World, European and Commonwealth Champion, Swimming

My advice would be to always work on your relationship with your coach. You want that communication, trust and respect as you develop as an athlete. For me I loved training, I had to work on my nerves and prep for racing. Keeping things simple. It wasn't life or death. I was just putting my hat and goggles on going for a swim. I had to learn to focus on the process and journey ... not the outcome.

Whatever your role in your team, work hard to show others that they can always rely on you to do your job.

You'll also likely encounter situations where trust between you and your team might not immediately be there. This is part and parcel of being around groups of people, where it can take time to develop. I've certainly encountered this circumstance in the past and it's important to have strategies in place to make sure your performance doesn't suffer as a result.

ELITE INSIGHT

Danny Holdcroft –
Head of Performance, BBSA (British Bobsleigh and Skeleton Association)

There is a lot of conversation about the coach/athlete relationship and how this should look. The honest answer from my experience is that it's very much determined by where an athlete is at in their journey and what is needed. Coaching children is a totally different mechanism to coaching elite athletes; however, the underlying factor that over-arches everything is people skills and a coach's ability to interact and sync with the athlete. A coach needs to have the ability to see a picture from multiple perspectives and the visionary capacity to sell a journey. But more importantly, communicate at a level that matches the ath-lete. Therefore when seeking out a coach, of course you should con-sider technical knowledge; however, this should be carefully balanced and in my opinion, very much second to people skills possessed.

A coach's role is to feed off the natural energy and drive of an athlete (however young), inspiring and captivating them to new heights of performance to follow a journey that will take them to whatever goal is set out.

For me as a coach that has worked with six-year-olds to the Olympic-level athletes, it is not easy as an individual to have success across varying age groups and levels. To do so requires a coach to need to reinvent themselves with every age group. Each athlete needs an environment to be themselves and allow their personality to shine, at the root of everything is enjoyment. The reason we normally become involved in the first place.

The coach's responsibility is to identify everyone's unique drivers and mould them to become the fuel to allow them to travel the so-called journey. A good coach will allow you to be yourself and give you guidance to develop your skills and abilities in your chosen sport.

Sport is all about people and two-way transactions. As an aspiring coach you grow and develop. It is fair to say that I have faced many personalities, some stronger and more forceful than mine. However, you have to try and find the mechanism to unlock the relationship to enable success.

There'll be occasions when you will have a dynamic that is not workable and you have to accept things will not work, however on the occasion when relationships click you get a push and a pull mentality that becomes a vehicle to success.

High performance is about boundaries & when a relationship is working, the opportunity to test limitations and boundaries and redefine them becomes a real possibility. This is when great things happen and performance can catapult to great heights. When you find an athlete that is prepared to put everything on the line to be successful & open to new direction, as I did with Amy, a coach can only be inspired to rise to the challenge & ensure that every intent by them is matched by you.

What you end up with is the removal of doubt and an inevitability for success. It is hard to frame in words, but in 2010, Vancouver, for Amy was the journey & from day one had an inevitable golden ending.

There's a lot of reasons why you might lack that immediate trust in a coach or a member of your wider team, but this isn't to say that the situation can't improve over time. You might work with a coach who perhaps doesn't have a significant history in the sport and your initial perception of them suffered as a result. I experienced this, but I still needed to respect them, do what they asked and not rush to judgement before they'd even began. If after some time it still isn't quite what you were hoping for then make the best of what they can do for you, continue to be respectful towards them and think carefully about personal accountability as discussed in the next section.

PERSONAL ACCOUNTABILITY

The most important consequence of the team/athlete relationship is your performance, after all. Try not to put the entirety of this on the shoulders of your coaches and your team. During the times when I didn't have complete faith in a coach I made sure I was still doing everything I possibly could to learn outside of that environment. I read more, I researched more, I spoke to as many people as I could to maintain my development and I started using a much stronger sense of personal responsibility and accountability.

Note to Self

"Take responsibility for your own performance, be in charge of your own dream".

ELITE INSIGHT

Hannah White –
World Record Holder, Sailor, Broadcaster, Adventurer:

The interesting thing about solo long-distance sailing is that you're on your own for such a long period of time. In normal life, you're so used to having confirmation from other people about the decisions you're making in life. This isn't the case in solo sailing. It's so much more difficult to make those decisions entirely by yourself and really having to own them. There's no one to blame, no one to use as a scapegoat and no one to use as a sounding board. This creates the feeling of huge pressure when you're out there doing that. You're there every single second of every single day, making every single decision and trying to keep yourself motivated without anyone to pick you up or bounce any ideas off. For a young athlete, particularly those in sports that aren't team based, this is a really important thing to think about. Even though I had a great team at home, I couldn't pick up the phone and call them every five minutes. This level of accountability wasn't taught to me at all, I simply had to make it up as I went along because it was essential to do so. I tried to immerse myself in the available knowledge as to how I could best prepare myself. I read books by Mike Golding and by Ellen Macarthur, trying to soak up as much as I possibly could from their experiences in the hope they'd be relevant to mine. But it's only on reflection now, looking back that there were so many other important skills that I wished I could have learnt at the early stages of my career. Be self-motivated and accountable to yourself to learn and develop as much as you possibly can.

Accountability was a key emphasis of the British Skeleton Team I was part of. We would have a big review at the start and end of each winter season in April and September, giving us the opportunity to get all of the staff and athletes in a room together to do a SWOT (strength, weaknesses, opportunities and threats) analysis. We'd go through each area of our sport, carry out the SWOT, then at the end of a few long days we would have our own new goals to work towards for the following summer and winter season. Importantly, we'd also have to sign an athlete agreement. This was an essential part of our accountability as it outlined our shared goals, vision and the rules within the team and sport. It was vital for the team cohesion that we all knew exactly what our role was, what was expected of us and what we should be achieving both individually and collectively.

STRENGTHS

★ Fast runner

★ Good at preparation

★ Loves training

★ Good concentration

WEAKNESSES

★ Negative thoughts

★ Gets anxious

★ Look at other... competitors too much

★ Bad back

SWOT

OPPORTUNITIES

★ Learns fast

★ New training camp to attend

★ Researching strength training

★ Take part in a potentiation study

THREATS

★ Not having enough time to train

★ Not having the best equipment

★ Not having enough money

★ Standing on feet too long at work all day.

> # Questions to ask yourself....

 STRENGTHS  Internal + Helpful

- What are you good at?
- What do you enjoy?

WEAKNESSESS  Internal + Harmful

- What areas do you need to develop?
- What are all the things you need to improve?

OPPORTUNITIES External + Helpful

- What resources are out these to help you?
- Who can you speak to for advice?

THREATS  External + Harmful

- What do you feel may stop you achieving your goals?
- What barriers are there ahead?

Really think about your own personal responsibility. Get yourself into exceptionally good habits from as early an age as you can and not just when it's directly related to your sport. You'll find your lifestyle away from the sport will contribute to the kind of athlete you are just as much as what you do during training and competition. Arrive on time, clear up after yourself, maintain and clean any equipment you use, don't lose equipment, be organised and be respectful to everyone. Accept the responsibility of what your role in the team is and do your utmost to achieve it. Everyone (including you) has a job to do and you have to trust each other that you'll all do it. Trust and accountability build over time within a team to the point when you know everyone is doing their job properly, this is all the more important in times of stress and top competition. Play your part.

> **TOP TIP:** Always be 5 minutes early to training, meetings and any team gathering.

ELITE INSIGHT

Heather Stanning MBE –
London 2012 and Rio De Janeiro 2016 Olympic Gold Medallist, Multiple World and European Champion, Rowing

From personal experience the value of the team is irreplaceable (for me it was crew mate and coach), they share the highs and lows, motivate you when you need that extra push and give you a reason to work that little bit harder ensuring you reach those goals.

FAMILY AND FRIENDS

Reaching the higher levels of sporting success is tough to achieve. You'll need to make sacrifices and you'll need to be dedicated. You'll also need the people closest to you. They might not get a badge or any kit that says they're part of the team, but your family and friends are still an essential part of your structure. Never underestimate the importance of this wider support team, away from those directly involved with your training and performance.

I was lucky in that my family and friends were always a massive support to me. My parents never pushed me, they supported me and helped me, driving me all over the place at crazy times in the morning so I could compete. Aside from their help with logistics (of which there was an awful lot), they along with my friends were also the people that knew me the best. I relied on them when I needed picking up if I felt low, to speak openly and honestly with me about any aspect of what I was doing. They might not have been able to help with advice on the technicalities of a particular corner at Altenberg ice track, but they could speak to me as Amy the person, not as Amy the athlete. They helped me to have a life outside of sport as well. It's important to switch off sometimes and give your mind and body a break from intense training and competition. This is where your friends and family can be so important.

Using the mantra that a happy athlete is a better athlete, don't ever forget those closest to you and their ability to help you with your overall well-being. This will have a direct impact on your performance.

TOP TIP: Think about what makes you happy: a good book, a funny movie, looking at a favourite photo or quote. Bring them with you when you are away on camps or competitions.

ELITE INSIGHT

Dame Sarah Storey –
Multiple World and Paralympic Champion, Cycling and Swimming

It is so hard as a parent to take a step back and let your child lead; allow them to make mistakes and find out things for themselves. This is a healthy process that builds resilience and fosters the independence needed to compete at the highest level. Being able to problem solve without support is a key part of being an athlete, but also having the humility of knowing when to ask for help creates a rounded person who can function within a team.

I was given the reins to my after-school activities from a young age and if I wanted to start a new club or sports group, my parents asked me whether it was logistically feasible. If there was a clash with something I was already doing they asked me how I would like to solve that. Inevitably I would ask about the chance of moving timings about to ensure everything fitted in, so it became perfectly normal that I would finish swim training and go straight to a table-tennis practice, or on to a cross-country race after a morning session in the pool at the weekend. Learning this element of time management also proved vital for balancing my GCSE and A level years which happened between my first Games in 1992 and second Games in 1996.

TEAMMATES

Your direct teammates are a big part of your performance and your mindset. In a team sport, you might rely on your teammates for your own performance, and in an individual sport, you might wear the same kit, but also compete against each other. Whichever it is, a cohesive team will outperform a divided one. But it's incredibly rare on any team that everyone will get on perfectly well with everyone else. Sometimes it's just inevitable that teammates will have a personality clash and it's how you handle this kind of situation that can help determine your team cohesion.

As soon as you feel like there's a situation that's affecting your performance, speak to people you trust, who might be able to mediate the situation, not necessarily teammates, but someone who could help you to constructively and positively do something about it. I always found this kind of issue difficult to deal with. I'm a very emotional person, feelings affect me and subsequently my performance. I worried about things, it made me stressed in comparison to those who might be able to just brush off such feelings. It was really important for my personality type to try and work through it constructively. Avoiding an issue won't make it go away and it'll mean you aren't getting the most out of your team. Always make sure that communication is a key element to how you work in a team.

Related to this, always remember to consider your own impact on team cohesion. You might not be best friends with everyone on your team, but you can always be polite, respectful and treat everyone with decency as a starting point. You'll find by doing this that your relationships throughout the team will be far better and so will your mentality and performance as a result.

That said, just because you compete directly with a teammate doesn't mean you need to see them as an enemy or a negative influence, it can and should be quite the opposite. I see how well it's worked with the current GB skeleton team where Laura Deas and Lizzy Yarnold have remained friends, despite competing against each other. They push each other on and help each other out all the time and they're each a part of the reasons they've had so much success in recent years.

Likewise with your rivals from other teams. You can still be fiercely competitive but also respectful, helpful and a team player. Two of my closest friends on the skeleton circuit were Anja Huber and Kerstin Szymkowiak of Germany, the other two medallists from my Olympic final. We were opponents when we were stood at the top of the ice track and we were competing for ourselves as individuals, but as soon as the competition was over, we were friends and we congratulated each other whatever the result. To this day we still message each other every year on our Medals Birthdays.

When you have rivals who you know are exceptionally good, it should always serve as motivation and fire to push yourself as hard as you possibly can. I can't help but think that Andy Murray became a much better tennis player because he was well aware he was in an era alongside Federer, Nadal and Djokovic. He must have felt it was verging on the impossible to beat these guys, but he always used the incredible level of his competitors to drive himself further on. If there'd only been one of Venus or Serena Williams growing up, would the other have been just as good? Or did they use the level of competition with the other to reach the heights they did?

> "THERE IS NO **BETTER RIVAL** THEN **YOURSELF**. PUSH **YOURSELF** TO YOUR **LIMITS**, AND **BEAT** YOUR **OWN PERFORMANCE** EVERY DAY, NOT SOMEONE ELSE'S. THEY WILL NOT MAKE YOU GO **FASTER**".

ELITE INSIGHT

Hannah White –
World Record Holder, Sailor, Broadcaster, Adventurer

In solo sailing, as well as racing against your competitors, you're also entirely reliant on them for your safety. If you get into trouble in the middle of the Atlantic, your nearest point of help is a competitor. There's very little shipping in the parts of the world we sail, at many points you're actually closer to a satellite in space than you are to land. This creates the need for a sort of "false friendship" where we stay in constant email contact with each other so we can share our experiences that can keep us safe, but on the other hand, you're also racing against them. It's a nice lesson in that we're fierce rivals, but we also really need each other.

Don't ever underestimate what you can learn from wider teams as well. I learnt a great deal from people from other sports who shared their experiences and knowledge that had a big impact on us in the skeleton team. I remember Jamie Staff, the gold medal–winning track cyclist who came to speak to us. He spoke a lot about mindset, about remaining laser focussed on your own job on race day. "Don't focus on others", "don't focus on anything other than what you've got to do", and "think logically, not emotionally". He taught me to focus on myself and only myself, not letting anything distract me. He used phrases like "why would anything go wrong just because it's race day". It's small pieces of advice like this that I could really think about, and it helped me handle my nerves and butterflies before an event, putting me in exactly the right frame of mind to perform.

We also had a team sport psychologist, Deidre Angelica, who was a big support in helping me understand those nervous feelings I was having. She taught me that they're just the same as the excited feelings and I just needed to reframe them in my mind. She drummed into me that nerves are a good thing. She helped me realise that my way of gaining confidence was by doing everything I physically and mentally could to prepare for events. The butterflies you feel in your tummy when you are excited about your birthday, Christmas or going on holiday are the same as when you are scared, nervous or anxious. It's just your mindset and attitude that has changed.

I'll never forget the great relationship I had with Chris Price, my sports physiotherapist who at the time worked for the English Institute of Sport (EIS). With all my knocks, bumps, multiple knee injuries and back issues, we spent a lot of time together as he treated all my problems!

In January 2009, only a year before the Olympic Games in Vancouver we were out in Konigssee, Germany. There is a beautiful lake there at the bottom of the Ice track. After training sessions, we were always advised to make up an ice bath (normally back at the hotel room) to help with muscle recovery. On this occasion, after a late evening sliding session, Chris suggested that I go into the then frozen lake instead, making it quicker than waiting until being back at the hotel. All the other athletes went back, but I decided to stay. I specifically remember his big boot having to smash the ice to make a hole for me to stand in (up to my waist). Chris was always encouraging and kept me on track with my end goals, even when I stood there shivering! I remember him saying, "When you are standing on that podium in Whistler, you will think back to times like this and be grateful that the discomfort and effort were all worthwhile".

Teamwork never has to stop at just your immediate team; there are always other sources, other people, other experiences and knowledge that you can use in your own sport. Always look to broaden your team and give yourself a much bigger opportunity to find other ways to help yourself as an athlete.

KNOW YOUR ROLE

In a team there needs to be a clear leader. High-performing teams need to have someone who has the right leadership qualities. This person needs to keep the team together, create the trust between everyone and a culture that enables everyone to do their job and carry out their role with confidence.

Having clear values and behaviours that everyone agrees to is really important. When the pressure is on at a competition, race or game you the individual and the team as a whole all need to rally together and stick to the values, especially in stressful, chaotic situations and moments.

Simply knowing your roles and responsibilities can make a huge difference to the team's overall performance. Knowing who you go to for each issue, problem or question keeps the athlete calm and in control when they're feeling flustered or stressed.

A great example of when all of this came together perfectly was at the Vancouver Olympics. On the second day of training the head ice coach, Micky Gruenberger, became ill. During pre-season camps, the team had all agreed that if anyone were to become ill you not only said it straightaway, but you took yourself away from the rest of the team and moved out of the team house, so that's what Micky did.

This didn't lead to any stress, worry or anxiety from the team or myself even though he was my main coach. Because of the prior planning, everyone knew what their new role was within the team to make sure all the gaps were covered and the athletes were kept happy. Everyone was relaxed and shifted to their new role easily.

Always ensure there's clarity in what your and everyone else's role in the team is.

DEALING WITH CONFLICT

You might have different coaches or team members for different elements of your sport, or for different levels of athletes. You might think you'd work better with a certain coach, but that coach might not be available because you're either too high up a level, or below the level that coach operates at. You might therefore not be with the coach who'd be your preference, sometimes you just have to get on with it, take responsibility and make the best of the situation.

The tricky side is if it gets to the stage where you *really* don't want to work with a particular coach, whether it's a personality clash or you don't like their methods at all and it's at the point where it's unworkable. Hopefully this doesn't happen to you, but it's possible. I've never been in the position where it's a case of "oh my goodness I just can't stand them" (thankfully!), but I've certainly had experiences where I felt we didn't have the right levels of communication, where I felt I wasn't able to speak freely and in a trusting environment where I knew I'd be taken seriously. If this happens, I'd advise you to look for some kind of mediator. Someone who you trust, but is separate from the direct coaching relationship (this could be a physio, a doctor, a nutritionist, anyone that's part of the team that you feel comfortable talking to) and you can discuss the issues with them. That mediator could then in turn speak to that certain coach. With me being shy and a little sensitive, when I did have issues with a coach, I never felt comfortable talking directly to them, so having someone I trust talking to them was a real help. Things may feel awkward at the beginning of these kinds of conversations, but eventually, in my situations it was invaluable. Between myself and my coach at the time, we eventually found a way that worked for both of us.

"BE **BRAVE** AND **SPEAK OUT.** IT'S YOUR **PERFORMANCE** THAT MATTERS, YOUR **GOALS** AND **DREAMS.** BEING HONEST ABOUT HOW YOU FEEL WILL THEN HAVE A **POSITIVE IMPACT** ON YOUR **PERFORMANCE**".

Any good coach will realise that situations like this are only a result of the athlete wanting their performance to improve. This is a gutsy thing for an athlete to do, but also really necessary. This is your life, your satisfaction and your performance. If you feel that something is affecting that, then take steps to improve things. Staying quiet and ignoring the issues won't make them better.

I was happy that throughout my career that cohesion was a priority for the British Skeleton Team, we were given various questionnaires to show how to handle someone with a different personality to ourselves. It helped to understand the personalities and preferences of people within the team. I found it really useful when they colour coded our traits, so you'd have the "red" people classified as more direct, fiery, cut to the chase types, then the polar opposite was your "green" person (me!), very sensitive, prefers longer conversations and feelings affect us more. In general terms, red and green people would be less compatible within a team, where red would think green is too fluffy and green would find red too abrasive. Then you've got your blues, who are very analytical and love facts, figures, detail and numbers, and finally your yellows who are your bubbly, carefree types. You'd also then imagine that yellows and blues wouldn't exactly be a great fit either. Clearly this isn't about putting people firmly into one category, we all have elements of each colour, just with higher levels of one over the other. I remember we did this colour test before the Turin games in 2006 and I found it really useful. It helped us greens to understand where a red was coming from, so I tried to just cut to the chase with the reds and they'd understand us more by taking some time to say, "Good morning, how are you" which helped us sensitive greens. It definitely helps you to understand how to work with different personalities, I know this from personal experience where my red/blue husband is married to me as his green/yellow wife!

Personality Colours

Everyone in your sport, team and organisation has a different personality. These can be explained really well using a color profile wheel. We can all have a mixture of all the colours, but some will be stronger and be your dominant colour. Understanding each other's colours will allow you all to get on much better as a team and therefore increase your performance.

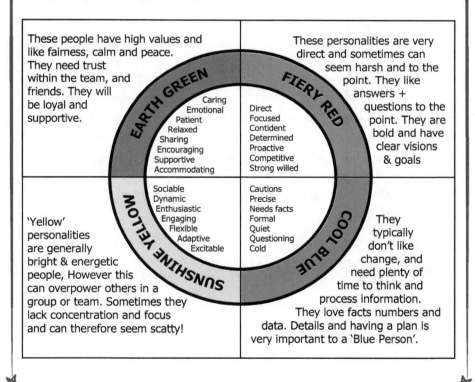

These people have high values and like fairness, calm and peace. They need trust within the team, and friends. They will be loyal and supportive.

These personalities are very direct and sometimes can seem harsh and to the point. They like answers + questions to the point. They are bold and have clear visions & goals

EARTH GREEN
Caring
Emotional
Patient
Relaxed
Sharing
Encouraging
Supportive
Accommodating

FIERY RED
Direct
Focused
Confident
Determined
Proactive
Competitive
Strong willed

SUNSHINE YELLOW
Sociable
Dynamic
Enthusiastic
Engaging
Flexible
Adaptive
Excitable

COOL BLUE
Cautions
Precise
Needs facts
Formal
Quiet
Questioning
Cold

'Yellow' personalities are generally bright & energetic people, However this can overpower others in a group or team. Sometimes they lack concentration and focus and can therefore seem scatty!

They typically don't like change, and need plenty of time to think and process information. They love facts numbers and data. Details and having a plan is very important to a 'Blue Person'.

It can be a real strength of a team that you have these different personality types working well together. I'd have coaches who were fantastic at studying the tracks, analysing all of our data in great detail, working out where I was losing time. This was so beneficial at the Olympics for me when I wanted to avoid all distractions and ideally avoid as much detail as possible. One of my coaches would go through the data, give me the information and then trusted me to get on with it.

Think about your own personality type, then think about how others prefer to be worked with and make efforts to adapt. Formulate an idea of what works best for you and use other team members with different skill sets to you to complement your strengths.

Your team members, in whatever role they play, are essential to your success. The extent to which they can help you will in certain ways be determined by how well you maximise the positives they bring to you, while minimizing the negatives.

You need your team, and they need you; remember, you all have a common goal.

ATHLETE IN FOCUS

Heather Fell –
2008 Beijing Olympic Silver Medallist, World and European Champion, Modern Pentathlon

How do you convert commitment and talent into medal success?

For me it was getting the buy-in from those around me, my team. That might sound odd as I was in an individual sport. At school I had my sights on making it as an Olympic swimmer, I gave it everything I had and I failed. However, all of that effort did not go to waste. On the surface I had become a very strong swimmer which would serve me well in my next sporting step but it went far deeper than that. I had learned how to push myself, how to balance a tough training regime but most importantly I had unknowingly convinced those around me I was serious about my future in sport.

My swim coach was one of the first to show his belief in me. A man of few words, he once told me, "You will make it". I was too scared to even ask what that meant but I knew he had faith in me as an athlete, even if at that early stage of my career I didn't. When I had to be honest with myself and admit I wasn't going to make it as a swimmer I questioned this comment and realised "making it" was open to my definition, and there was still an opportunity to prove him right.

There was a significant amount of understanding and support I required from my coaches, teachers, parents and friends in order to train for five sports whilst still keeping up with my school work. I could never have enough time or energy to give to any area. Add in the fact that each individual sport coach would want more of my commitment and dedication it became a challenge in self-management. Ultimately they were all there to help me reach my potential; however, I was responsible for my own actions and my future. I soon learnt that there was no magic short-cut: the work had to go in a long time before the results would come out.

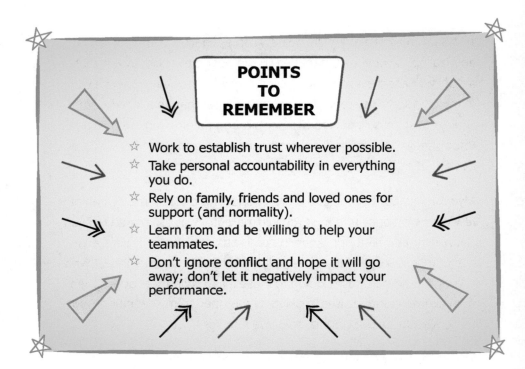

POINTS TO REMEMBER

☆ Work to establish trust wherever possible.

☆ Take personal accountability in everything you do.

☆ Rely on family, friends and loved ones for support (and normality).

☆ Learn from and be willing to help your teammates.

☆ Don't ignore conflict and hope it will go away; don't let it negatively impact your performance.

5 Goals

A dream or a goal is your desire and aspiration to achieve something that means a lot to you. Something that you feel deep inside; it comes from your heart – it's a passion, a fire in the pit of your belly.

They are there in the back of your mind daily, they may go away for a while if life turns busy and other things get in the way but deep down they never leave you until you manage to achieve them. That passion and fire then need to be channelled in a way that is meaningful to your progress.

If you have a dream and create a goal and then achieve it, the very next thing you want to do is to create a higher goal and a higher dream. When you achieve that one you keep aiming higher and higher. If you are full of a passion and desire, you just need to give that a direction and you can achieve something magical. This chapter explains how you can do that.

In sport, the word "dream" usually gets changed into the word "goal". This is the switch from a thought process that might be "I want to break the world record for the 100 m" to "What do I need to do to break the world record for the 100m?" Goals play such an important part in motivating any athlete. Every champion, world record holder, Olympian or anyone who has been successful in sport, whether a swimmer, netballer, rugby player, footballer or runner, sets goals.

Dreams and goals all evolve. They will start small in the heart of a child and grow bigger by the time they enter teenage years.

My Dream Is.....

- **What is your big dream?**

- **What do you want to do?**

- **What do you hope to achieve?**

When I think back to myself, I was part of an athletics team from the age of 13 to 17. I loved doing all events, the 80-metre hurdles, 100-metre, 200-metre and then eventually the 400-metre races. I remember watching Sally Gunnell win her gold medal in the 400-metre hurdles at the Barcelona Olympics in 1992 when I was 10 years old.

Watching her hold the Union Jack flag around her shoulders as she walked around the stadium after the race. As she stood on the podium collecting her medal and flowers I remember thinking to myself – I wonder what it feels like to know you are the best in the world, that you are the fastest in the race.

What would it feel like to stand on the very top of the podium singing your national anthem? I guess for me this memory never really left me and maybe that's where the start of my dream came from. The better I got at sport, the more those dreams evolved into practical goals.

Note to self
Dream BIG
set GOALS
Take ACTION

I started to set myself goals of what I wanted to achieve in the gym, my weight training, my sprint times and then my times down the ice track. My mindset had changed.

Race by race, year by year, my goalposts started to move until I knew I had my eyes set on the Olympics.

In 2006 it was the Turin Winter Olympic Games. We knew as a nation that we only had one place in the women's team and two places for the men. I wanted that space, I wanted to be the one that went to compete. I felt like if everything went my way I was good enough to go and get picked for the team.

The only way I could be picked was to be the top ranked British girl during the races beforehand. There were eight World Cup races to qualify myself and be ranked the highest Brit. However with every race I was always a few places behind my fellow Brit and the realisation that I would not compete at these Olympics soon hit me. This setback, although painful, motivated me to re-evaluate. Right then, Amy, the Olympics is still my dream; I know how hard it's going to be to make it, so what am I going to do to achieve it?

WRITE DOWN YOUR GOALS

It's very important to sit down and work out what it is you want to achieve. What's the fire in your belly? What's your passion? What's going to motivate you to turn up to training every single day? What's going to drive you? You need to come up with your own goals.

They need to be meaningful and exactly right for you.

Then they need to be written down.

Once they are on a piece of paper (or screen!), you'll develop a sense of commitment and that stronger need to achieve them.

PERFORMANCE SPECIFIC GOAL SETTING

Here is a very sport and performance specific way of keeping track of goals, results and targets. This is a great way to record how well you are doing.

EVENT	GOAL RESULT NEEDED	ACTUAL RESULT	FACTORS INFLUENCING RESULT
1. Selection Race	Top 3	2nd	Felt prepared and focused. Trained well in the lead up.
2. School Football trials	Be in top 10	Got 1st reserve	Was very nervous. Felt tense. Need to control my nerves.
3.			
4.			
5.			
6.			

TASK ⟶ **Fill out chart with upcoming events + races. Then set new goals with the information.**

DREAM BIG

Take personal responsibility for your own destiny and place your future in your own hands. I truly believe that you need to have that drive from within yourself. It doesn't matter how much your parents, teachers, friends or coaches want you to achieve something and believe you can. Unless you feel it and want it yourself, you'll either end up giving up on the way or never quite making it because you haven't ever made that decision yourself.

Ask yourself some questions, what would you do in your wildest dreams if there are no barriers, no limitations, if money or resources were no problem?

What do *you* get excited about that makes *you* happy?

Then think "what am I going to do about it?"

MAKE YOUR GOALS CLEAR

You need to have clear goals with a structured timeframe that everyone else involved with your journey from coaches, parents, loved ones and teachers can see and have some level of input into.

There will be setbacks and moments of feeling like you're treading water during injuries, illness or other issues that may come. This can make it a really hard time for you to motivate yourself. By having clear goals you can help yourself stay on the right path and keep your behaviours positive and moving forward.

Clear goals need to be planned out, to the point where you can set out your very first goal "write down my goals clearly!"

ELITE INSIGHT

Jason Fox –
Former Special Forces Soldier, Television Presenter, Mental Health Advocate, Podcast Host

If you've done a good job at the visualisation thing, with regard your desire to get to a goal, whether it's a gold medal or selection for a team, if you really believe in your ability to do that, then every time along the way it gets tough, that becomes your focus again. It slips back to the front of your head & that's what gives you the determination to keep smashing out whatever it is you need to.

EMPHASISE CONSTANT ACHIEVEMENT

One of the most important things about goal setting is making sure that they are realistic and achievable. There is a very fine balance between aiming high and aiming for something out of your reach. It's really important to put smaller stepping stones in place, so you can constantly achieve and constantly improve.

Too many young athletes set huge dream goals for themselves and want to reach them too quickly. This can (and will) lead to disappointment after disappointment and never gives you the chance to build up the confidence you need to be able to achieve them further into the future.

Think of a multi-event athlete like Jessica Ennis-Hill. Winning the Olympic heptathlon may well have been her "dream", but to achieve this, she would have had to set out small goals for every event she competed in. She'd have broken it down and had plans like "this year I want to achieve a personal best in the hurdles" or "I want a top three finish in the javelin". If she'd have aimed to win every event of every heptathlon she competed in, she'd likely have been disappointed.

Every sport can be broken down into many different pieces. A footballer has to think about cardio fitness, ball skills, game tactics, position-specific strength training, left foot, right foot, heading and many more. Rather than trying to be the best in the world at all of those things immediately, the footballer can take each one step by step and put in place a mindset of constant improvement of each skill. They can track their progress, they can see themselves being further ahead this year than they were last year, they can keep pushing themselves out of their comfort zone and after years of doing this, they can eventually hit their peak.

Constant achievement will eventually see you reach your full potential.

LIFE BALANCE PIE CHART

This is a great task to do to rank yourself in the different areas of your life. you can do a general life chart and / or a sport specific.

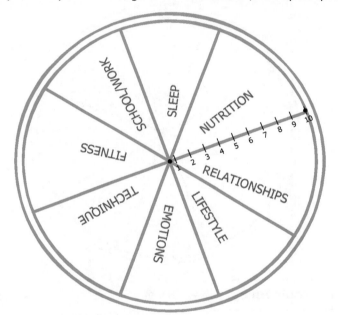

How : 1. Choose specific topics important to you.

2. Rank yourself 1-10 on each topic.

3. You will see a clear result on what you will need to improve on.

4. Write NEW GOALS on the topics that need the most work.

5. Re-evaluate every 3|6|9|12 months.

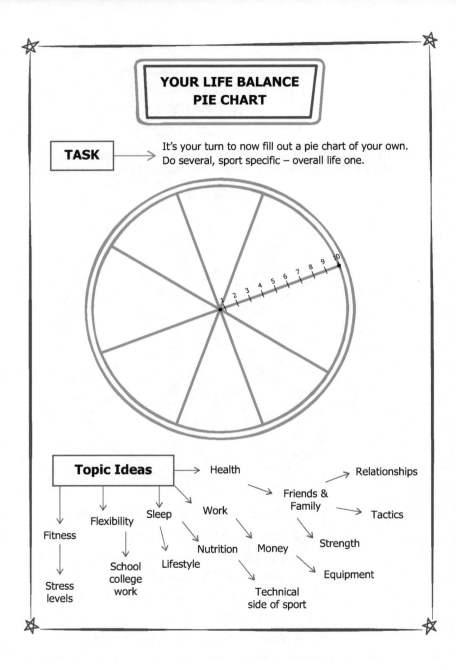

YOUR LIFE BALANCE PIE CHART

TASK → It's your turn to now fill out a pie chart of your own. Do several, sport specific – overall life one.

Topic Ideas → Health

Relationships

Friends & Family

Tactics

Fitness

Flexibility Sleep Work

Strength

Nutrition Money

Stress levels

School college work Lifestyle

Equipment

Technical side of sport

DIFFERENT KINDS OF GOALS

There are three different types of goals that are all equally important and won't work without the other. They all play a very different role in your training.

1. Outcome goals – These keep you motivated and give you a sense of direction. These are long-term, future-gazing goals: "I want to win an Olympic medal"; "I want to go to a Commonwealth Games"; "I want to represent my county or my country".

    These are goals that focus on the competitive results of the activity/sport/game.

    REMEMBER: You may not have total control over these goals.

2. Performance goals – You'll only achieve your outcome goals *if* you focus and achieve your performance goals. These need to be measurable: "I need to sprint 100 metres in 11 seconds". "I need to get a top 3 finish". "I need to be a starting player in my team".

    These are goals that focus on achieving results that are independent of the other competitors or teams.

    REMEMBER: You mostly have control over these goals.

3. Process goals – These address how you achieve your performance goals. They may be around your technique and how you run, focussing on a particular aspect like driving your

knees higher or striding out further. Your strength training goals (how heavy can I be lifting) or your nutrition goals.

These are goals that focus on the task that must take place to show improvements in your sport.

REMEMBER: You have complete control over these goals.

When you have your big outcome goal written down you then need to work backwards, year by year, month by month, week by week, day by day.

This will become a step-by-step guide to follow that you feel you can achieve every day. They'll also maintain your focus on that main end goal.

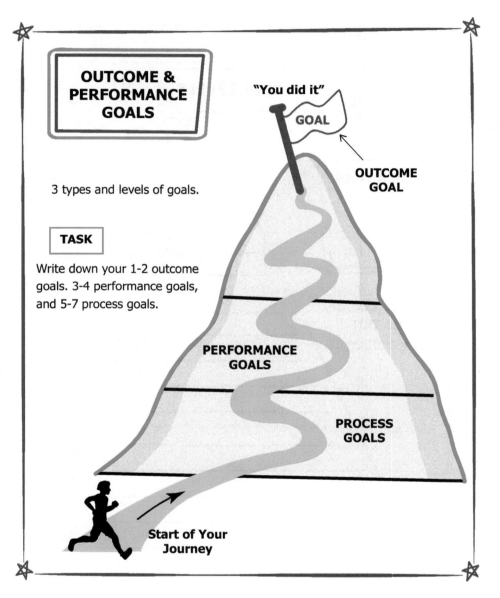

OUTCOME & PERFORMANCE GOALS

"You did it"

GOAL

OUTCOME GOAL

3 types and levels of goals.

TASK

Write down your 1-2 outcome goals. 3-4 performance goals, and 5-7 process goals.

PERFORMANCE GOALS

PROCESS GOALS

Start of Your Journey

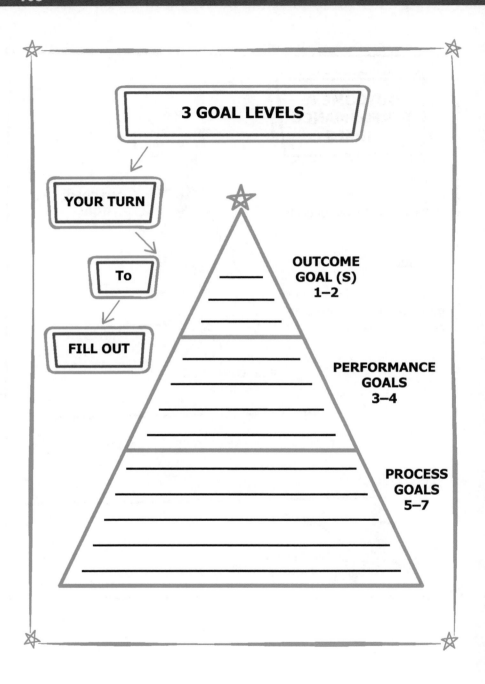

MY EXAMPLE: OUTCOME GOAL – Go to Vancouver Olympics and win a medal.

PERFORMANCE GOAL – Be ranked in the top 2 in Britain in the year leading up to the Olympics. Come in top 2 at selection races at the start of the season. Be top 3 ranked in the world at my push times.

PROCESS GOAL – Drive my knees and "eat up the ground" during my push sessions. Lift another 50 kg in my leg press exercises.

BE FLEXIBLE

The outcome goals are going to keep you motivated and give you that sense of direction and constant achievement knowing you're on the right path. You need to find the right balance between making sure the goals you set are realistic and achievable. Make sure they aren't too easy otherwise you'll lose motivation and it won't mean enough when you achieve them.

You also need to be flexible and ensure these goalposts can be shifted and moved. You might suddenly have a peak in performance a lot earlier than you were expecting and may reach some of the bigger goals a lot quicker. If so, change them, improve them, stretch yourself, but always in an achievable manner.

Some years you might not achieve the goals that you set out to. When that happens (and it will), you need to work out why and what went wrong. Is there something obvious that sticks out, or do you need to go through every area and find out which can be improved on? How much heartbreak and disappointment did Dame Kelly Holmes endure before she won double Olympic gold in Athens in 2004? The answer is an awful lot. Each time she suffered an injury or a bad race, she used this as a way to learn and, most importantly, to set new goals. How could she reduce the amount of injuries she was having? Was there more she could be doing tactically in a race? She knew she had the talent, ability and work ethic, so why the disappointments? Learning from setbacks is absolutely key in your goal setting. That's why flexibility is essential. The more experience you gather in your sport, the more you can tweak your goals towards your dream.

As an athlete in British Skeleton we would meet up every 6 months to go through the team goals and our individual goals. We would have to talk about them with our performance coaches, the ice coach, the strength coach and then the performance director. Everyone would have to agree on them and then they would be written down for everyone to see. These were really important times, a time to monitor performance and look at old performances and results. We'd then look ahead to set new goals and to re-evaluate what we wanted to achieve.

SMART GOALS

There's a reason why SMART goals have been so popular in sport, business and so many other aspects of life. That's largely as they're generally very effective if you stick to them. Here's a description of each, for you, now think about how you can relate them to every aspect of your goal setting (then, of course, write them down!).

S – SPECIFIC

What do I want to accomplish? What's my goal? What am I aiming for? Why do I want to accomplish this? What are the requirements? What are the barriers in the way?

M – MEASURABLE

How can I measure my goals? Can you time or write down a unit to record your goal? How will I measure my progress? How will I know when the goal is accomplished and achieved?

A – ACHIEVABLE

How can the goal be achieved? What are the logical steps I should take? Have I made it possible for me to achieve?

R – REALISTIC/RELEVANT

Is this a worthwhile goal? Is this the right time? Do I have the necessary resources to accomplish this goal? Is this in line with my long-term objectives? Is this goal possible for me to achieve?

T – TIME BOUND

How long will it take for me to achieve this goal? When is the competition? When am I going to work on this goal? What is my deadline?

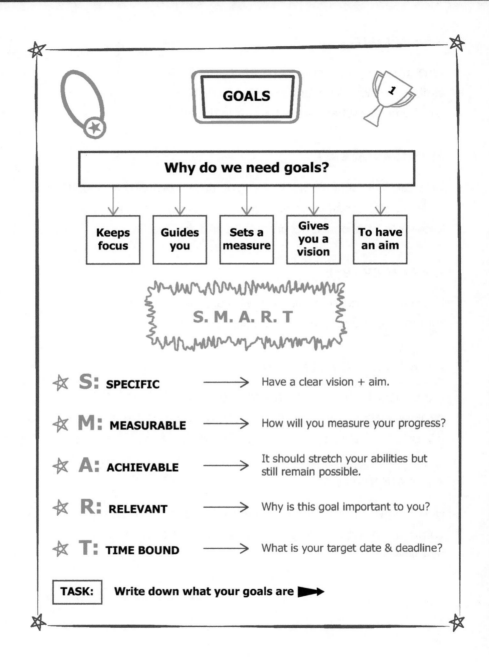

GOALS

1

Why do we need goals?

| Keeps focus | Guides you | Sets a measure | Gives you a vision | To have an aim |

S. M. A. R. T

⭐ **S:** SPECIFIC ⟶ Have a clear vision + aim.

⭐ **M:** MEASURABLE ⟶ How will you measure your progress?

⭐ **A:** ACHIEVABLE ⟶ It should stretch your abilities but still remain possible.

⭐ **R:** RELEVANT ⟶ Why is this goal important to you?

⭐ **T:** TIME BOUND ⟶ What is your target date & deadline?

TASK: **Write down what your goals are** ▶▶

YOUR GOALS

TASK ⟶ Using the life balance pie chart results, start using the SMART goals tool to write down what you want to achieve and aim towards. Do this for each "pie" of your chart.

⟶ You can re-write and re-evaluate these any time.

✪ **S:** _____

✪ **M:** _____

✪ **A:** _____

✪ **R:** _____

✪ **T:** _____

POST-EVENT BLUES

After a big event it can be normal to feel a dose of the blues and a little deflated.

When a competition ends, after a huge build-up and preparation period that may have lasted months and even years, you return home to your "normal life". You can feel like you no longer have a big goal to aim for anymore.

Suddenly that structure and direction have gone. Depression, anxiety and withdrawal can occur with the loss of the daily structure and commitments that were driving your life towards a major goal.

You need to be psychologically prepared for this potential comedown. My advice to you is to not fight the feeling. You are going to feel a bit of a down, you may not feel as happy as you did, but you need to give yourself time to recover, emotionally and physically.

Be prepared to feel this feeling; sometimes it lasts a few days, a week or even months. It can vary from person to person.

If this "low" continues for too long, or becomes something deeper, make sure you speak to your friends, family, a coach or a psychologist; they can step in to provide extra support you need.

When you feel ready, it's time to set some new goals.

TALENT ISN'T EVERYTHING

You may very well have a real talent for a sport and a big dream to achieve great things in it. That's wonderful, but you'll run the risk of not fulfilling this talent or achieving that dream if you don't have a plan. How do you know if you're progressing? If you're not, why not? Are you stretching yourself enough, or too much? Do you have a clear vision of what you want to do or how you're going to do it? If the answer to any of these questions is "I'm not sure" then you need to change from being a "dreamer" to being a "dreamer with a plan" that's a seriously powerful combination.

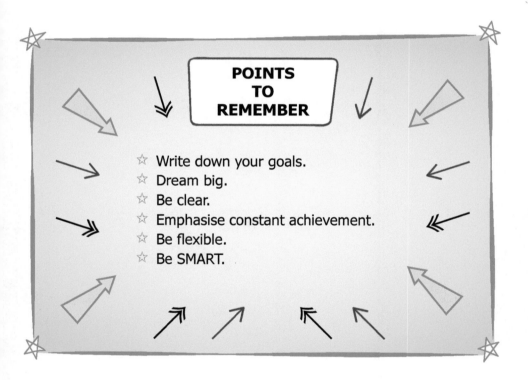

POINTS TO REMEMBER

☆ Write down your goals.
☆ Dream big.
☆ Be clear.
☆ Emphasise constant achievement.
☆ Be flexible.
☆ Be SMART.

6 Mindset

Training your body is a simple concept, if you have dedication, commitment, you train smartly, you eat well and you sleep well, your body will improve. But is this case with the mind? Can you work on your thought processes? Can you change and improve how you frame certain situations? Can you learn to deal with success and failure in a way that improves your performance?

The answer is yes you can, and it's equally important as your physical training.

In this chapter you'll learn how to work with the uniqueness of your own mind, how to manage your nerves, how to think logically rather than emotionally, how to improve your confidence and your motivation, and, finally, I'll be letting you into a secret as to what I think my superpower was that was perhaps the most important reason I achieved what I did.

ELITE INSIGHT

Jade Jones OBE –
Double Olympic Champion, London 2012 and Rio De Janeiro 2016, World Champion and European Champion, Taekwondo

For me the mind is so important in elite sport. When you are at the very top, the physical attributes are all very similar so the mental game is what makes the difference between winning a gold and just missing out. A lot of people neglect this and don't think it's important, but it is a skill and needs lots of training too. The best athletes have the ability to perform at their very best when they are under the ultimate pressure while others panic and underperform. Each could have the same physical skills but very different mental skills.

LEARN WHAT WORKS FOR YOU

People are different; they have different physical attributes and different mental attributes. Developing the right mindset is about finding the best way for *yourself* to perform at your best. It's unique to you and you'll only find it through gaining experience. This is another great example of taking the positives from a negative situation. Don't beat yourself up if you felt like you weren't in the right frame of mind before a competition and it affected your performance. This is a good thing, you've learnt what doesn't work. Next time you'll do something differently until you get to the point of knowing exactly what works for you. When you find this (and you will), hone it, build on it and constantly improve it.

> **TOP TIP:** Keep a notebook, and write down what actions or thoughts you did or had that you felt didn't work. Then write down how you could change those thoughts and actions for the next race, or competition.

It took me a long time to discover what worked best for me and my personality. Before a big competition, I realised that I didn't want to just sit in silence and focus my entire mind on what was about to happen. I liked a small amount of distraction, to relax my mind and avoid being too tense.

I was once lucky enough to be on the grid immediately before the start of a formula one race in 2011. The drivers were in their cars, and as you can imagine, the atmosphere was a mixture of tension, excitement and anticipation. I had the unique opportunity to speak with Michael Schumacher as he sat in his car. I asked him about his pre-race mindset, coping with nerves and getting into the right head space. With Michael's reputation as an intense, laser focussed and steely driver, you may have expected him to be understandably unwilling to engage in a conversation with anyone, let alone a random skeleton athlete! He was quite the opposite: he said he welcomed the opportunity for a little bit of distraction, and he wanted to feel calm and relaxed rather than over-emotional. Having a chat with someone unconnected to his team or the race helped him with this. This really resonated with me as I felt the same before a competition. I would read books, watch films, have a coffee with a friend, anything to feel relaxed and calm and not spend too much mental energy on over-thinking the event.

TOP TIP: Create your "happy place" before a competition. Have people and things around you that make you feel calm, happy and safe.

Think about the start line of a top-level 100-metre race just before the athletes step onto their blocks. Then take note of the different ways the individual competitors get themselves in their optimal mental zone. Some will be steely eyed, staring intently down their lane as though nothing else in the world existed. Others will be psyching themselves up, jumping up and down, talking to themselves, slapping their legs and face and doing everything they can to get the adrenalin pumping, ready to explode. Then if you're Usain Bolt, you're fist-bumping the kit carriers, smoothing out your eyebrows and generally looking as relaxed as someone who's having a bit of fun with their friends.

None of these styles is necessarily right or wrong for everyone. You wouldn't tell Usain Bolt that he should be more focussed and intense on the start line because it wouldn't work for him. Similarly, you wouldn't tell one of the more intense, aggressive athletes that if they lighten up and be more like Bolt, then they'd run faster. These are elite athletes who've developed phenomenal mental skills over many years and found what works for them individually. Do the same, but be patient and don't expect instant knowledge of your unique, optimal mental zone. Failures are fantastic lessons.

Note to Self

"Learn to like your failures. Every failure will teach you to become a better athlete".

MANAGE YOUR NERVES

Feeling nervous is inevitable; every competitor has felt those butterflies right before they're about to compete, no matter how relaxed they may outwardly seem. You'll often hear advice of "don't be nervous", which in itself is fine, but I'd frame it differently and say it's about how you use that nervous feeling, rather than trying to suppress it. When I was competing I had to deal with a mixture of nerves based on the pressure to succeed, as well as the nerves involved with being in such a dangerous and high adrenaline sport. If I hadn't developed mechanisms to maintain high performance in high pressure situations then I wouldn't have stood a chance. Luckily with experience, some great advice from sport psychologists and coaches, I learnt how to use the inevitable nerves to my advantage.

I learnt that the feeling of butterflies in the belly is precisely the same physical reaction you get when you're excited. Knowing this gave me the tools to change my thought process before a competition. Instead of thinking to myself "I'm so nervous", I thought, "I'm so excited to race; I can't wait to see what happens". I said it over and over to myself, using positive self-talk "I'm so excited". Have a watch of YouTube when I was stood at the top of the ice track at the 2010 Olympics. I can tell you exactly what I was thinking: "I'm the best athlete on this track and they're going to have to beat me". This is why we see so many elite competitors across every sport talking to themselves before a competition. "I can't lose"; "I've got this"; "I'm the best"; "I'm the greatest". There's a reason why you won't often (if ever!) see them using phrases like "I'm so nervous" or "I'm terrified". Negative self-talk like this is a sure way to let your nerves get the better of you and have a seriously negative effect on your performance.

Did Usain Bolt joke around and play to the crowd before big races entirely because he *was* so relaxed? Or was there an element of him *telling himself* that he felt relaxed, because he knew that he ran faster when he wasn't feeling tense or nervous?

When you control and reframe your nerves, you turn them into a positive. So the next time someone asks you if you're feeling nervous before a match or competition, what will you say in reply? "Yes, I'm terrified", or "No, I'm excited"?

THINK LOGICALLY, NOT EMOTIONALLY

As I said earlier in the book, I'm quite a sensitive and emotional person. If I'd let this side of me dominate my thought process during a competition, then I wouldn't have been able to perform at my best. This can be easier said than done and again; it took me a long time to learn how to optimise it. The concept has a lot of similarities with managing your nerves in that the way you frame your thoughts can have a big impact on the way you perform. I had to make a lot of mental mistakes in my early career before I realised just how much better I felt in myself by thinking logically rather than emotionally.

ELITE INSIGHT

Jason Fox –
Former Special Forces Soldier, Television Presenter, Mental Health Advocate, Podcast Host

Without sounding like a hippy, everything I used to do (and still do now) was around visualization. I think about the feeling at the end of a challenge of some sort, of succeeding. Whether you're aiming at getting selected for a team or you're trying to pass a challenge of some kind, visualise the positive outcome. I really embedded the concept of visualisation in my head. I didn't even realise I was doing it until now when I look back on it.

On the day of a challenge of any sort, I'd push the thought of the over-all challenge that might last a long time aside, then literally dealt with every second as it presented itself. I didn't even worry about the evening. If I woke up in the morning I just worried about the next thirty minutes, then the next thirty minutes. I didn't worry about cleaning my kit and getting ready for the next day. I didn't need to worry about that because I wasn't there yet.

It's about focussing on the skillset, then the mindset. It's about living in the moment. If I thought about SAS selection in its entirety, I'd have just freaked myself out. There's so many phases to it; it goes on for nine months, but what's the point in worrying about something that's three months down the line? You're not even there.

For me, it's about living life like an eighteen-month-old child. The child doesn't care about five minutes in front of it; it doesn't care if it fell over and hurt itself two minutes before; it just explores the moment that it's in. I was basically giving myself an excuse for being a toddler!

One of my biggest mistakes was to put too much emphasis on focussing my thoughts on what my competitors were doing. If someone did a faster run than me I thought about what training they must be doing? What's their secret? What do they know that I don't? Do they have a magic ingredient that I've missed? I found myself looking at their kit, their demeanour and how they prepare, watching their performances intently. If an athlete went before me and achieved a really fast run it affected me. I immediately thought, "Oh no", and wondered how on earth could I go faster than that?

These are examples of emotional rather than logical thinking. When I learnt to think logically, particularly in high pressure situations then my thought processes became far more positive and helpful. I say "helpful" because my emotional thought processes were proving highly "unhelpful". What would I gain by feeling stressed about the athlete(s) before me getting fast times? Nothing. What would I gain by worrying about what a competitor has been doing in training? Nothing. What would I gain by thinking the weather conditions might change for my run as oppose to someone else's? Nothing.

**LOGICAL
VS
EMOTIONAL THINKING**

**LOGICAL
THINKING BRAIN
THOUGHTS + WORDS**

**EMOTIONAL THINKING
BRAIN THOUGHTS +
WORDS**

Stable	**Target**	**Goals**	**Process**

Bad	**Negative**	**Not reliable**	**Things go wrong**

- **"Mistakes are good"**

- **"The butterflies are a good, excited feeling"**

- **"I have great process goals to work through"**

- **"I have prepared well"**

- **"Graphs from training show I'm on form".**

- **"I'm rubbish + slow"**

- **"I may make a mistake"**

- **"They are all so much faster than me".**

- **"Why can't I do it today?".**

- **"Its not fair".**

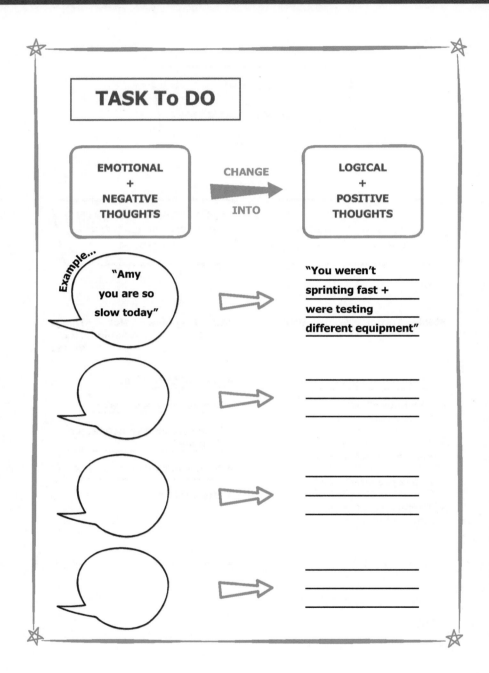

When I realised that I needed to look at each situation logically, then I learnt that by focussing much more on *myself* than others, I was building a mindset of *controlling the controllables*. Had I done everything in my own training to do the best I possibly could? Yes. Does another athlete's run affect how mine is going to go? No. What can I do about the weather? Nothing. Was it helpful for me to think about anything else other than being the best athlete I possibly can be on the day of a competition? No.

If I felt myself slipping into an unhelpfully negative thought process I consciously tried to change what I was thinking. I tried to stop thinking in terms of the word "if": "what if I slip?", "what if I crash?", "what if I mess up turn 1?" and "what if I don't do well?"

I talked to myself: "Amy, re-focus". I thought about how I was going to hold my sled, how I was going to explode from the start line, how I need to breathe, what my goals for the run are.

ELITE INSIGHT

Tanya Streeter –
World Champion and former record holder freediver.
Broadcaster, Adventurer, Environmentalist

Before every dive, be it a training dive, a competition dive or a world record attempt, I put my mind through the same paces. It's worth noting that despite breaking 10 world records in an extreme sport that continues to baffle the minds of medical professionals, scientists and regular people alike, I am no different to anybody else when it comes to negative self-talk. I've always envisaged it as having a devil on one shoulder whispering negative thoughts into my ear, and an angel on the other shoulder just telling me to keep trying. The angel never really said much else than that, but it was just enough to help me ignore the devil. "Just try. Just see what you can do", the angel would whisper. Just those simple words against the many from the devil. "You didn't sleep well enough. You didn't train hard enough. You didn't eat properly. You aren't hydrated enough. You don't deserve to succeed. You don't know what's going to happen to your body down there. You're scared of the dark. You're scared to fail. You're scared to succeed". That devil would never shut up! Once I realized that all I had to do was try, and rely on my innate mammalian human physiology, I knew above everything else that if it wasn't something physical stopping me from going deeper than it was just something mental. And was I going to make my mind my weapon or my weakness? It was a choice. It was a choice that depended heavily on self-integrity. Could I lie to myself? Could I tell myself I didn't eat well enough? Or train hard enough? Or deserve to succeed? Or could I believe that I had done enough and just see how far that "enough" would take me? It would be so much easier, down there, alone on the rope, hundreds of feet away from the surface and the people waiting for me, to turn away from my fear and create excuses to tell myself and my team. To turn around and head back to the surface. But every time I chose the harder option of staring down my fear and trying that little bit harder. And diving deeper. Deeper into my own strength and courage. And all because I made a choice. I made my mind my weapon. That devil didn't stand a chance.

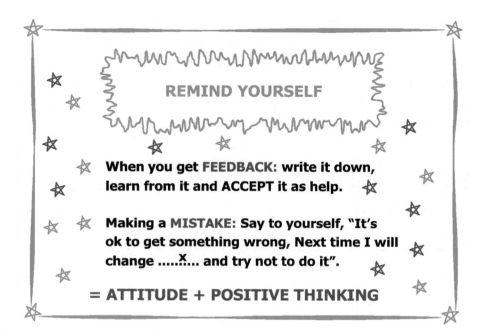

REMIND YOURSELF

When you get **FEEDBACK**: write it down, learn from it and **ACCEPT** it as help.

Making a **MISTAKE**: Say to yourself, "It's ok to get something wrong, Next time I will change .....X... and try not to do it".

= ATTITUDE + POSITIVE THINKING

Challenge yourself – Is your thinking helping you focus and achieve your goals? Is it helpful in the here and now? If it isn't, learn to refocus on what is.

ELITE INSIGHT

Hannah White –
World Record Holder, Sailor, Broadcaster, Adventurer

I remember the second time I did a transatlantic race. I had a message to say that not only was I was winning, but I was on course for the world record. Suddenly the weather just shut down entirely and there was no wind between me and the finish line, for days. I remember being incredibly upset at the time, but looking back, I wonder what on earth I was worrying about; there was nothing I could do about it. My sport taught me to be a realist. I look at the facts for what they are. I'm neither overly negative about them nor overly positive. I treat them for what they are and what I need to do. There's no point in worrying about things you can't control, you just have to focus entirely on what you're doing. Drown out the noise. I wasn't born with this skill; it's definitely something I've developed over time. I learnt to look back at what I'd done in previous races and analysed what I did wrong and gradually gained the experience to know this. I hope you can start earlier!

Note to Self

"Don't believe everything you think. LOOK at the facts and data".

CONFIDENCE

Confidence comes in many different forms for different people. If you ask people today to name confident athletes of the past or present you might hear examples like Muhammad Ali, Cristiano Ronaldo, Claressa Shields, Usain Bolt, Serena Williams or Simone Biles. Was it their confidence in themselves that drove them to the heights they achieved (or are still achieving)? It certainly worked for them, but it asks the question as to exactly what confidence is and where does it come from. Do you have to be outrageously certain of your own ability in the way that Muhammad Ali expressed to be considered confident? You'd rarely hear Serena Williams or Simone Biles boasting about their greatness, despite their extreme levels of dominance in their sports and their clear confidence in themselves.

Using myself as an example, I've never been the most outwardly confident person in the world and had to work really hard to learn how confidence can manifest itself and help my performance. However unlikely it may seem, I can see similarities in the confidence levels of those that show it (Muhammad Ali) and those that don't (Amy Williams!). If you look at confidence purely as an outward expression of your greatness, then my tenuous comparison to one of the greatest boxers of all time ends fairly quickly. But if you look at confidence as *the expectation that something is going to happen*, then you can start to think about how you can develop your own form of confidence. As someone with a lack of it, I knew that in order to feel confident, I had to have done every possible piece of preparation I could to the highest possible standard. Every box had to be ticked, I had to be certain that on that day, I was the best possible athlete I could be.

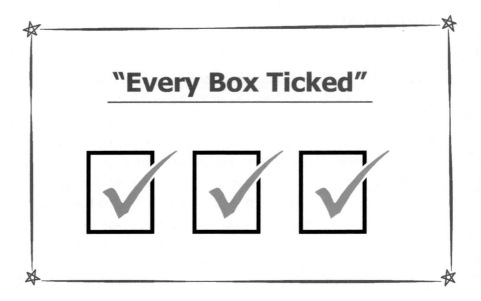

"Every Box Ticked"

This was the feeling I had when I was at the Olympics in 2010. For years, I'd done everything right, I'd left no stone unturned, every decision I made was for this one competition. My training was good, my data was good, my form was good and my results had been good in the lead up to the event, and for these reasons, I'd removed all the reasons for self-doubt. Dare I say it, I was actually confident. Whether you're naturally gregarious and confident, or like me, inwardly lacking in confidence, there are steps you can take to improve it.

ELITE INSIGHT

Heather Stanning MBE –
London 2012 and Rio De Janeiro 2016 Olympic Gold Medallist,
Multiple World and European champion, Rowing

Confidence can be tough to harness at time. When I needed to rein-
force my confidence I used to use objective evidence, such as remind-
ing myself of some of the PBs I'd achieved or a good race I'd had. By
drawing on things I had done and achieved reminded me of what I
was capable of.

The final point I'd make about confidence that leads on from the
expectation of success is that it should be based on something
real. Confidence by itself isn't enough to make you successful. I
feel like it was to my advantage that I wasn't naturally confident,
because it meant that I had to do serious work in order to remove
self-doubt. Over-confidence can be just as damaging to your
maximising potential as under-confidence can be.

Do the work, be humble and have your confidence be based
on what you've been doing rather than thinking what you can
just do. Never doubt the amount of behind-the-scenes work
done by Muhammad Ali, Cristiano Ronaldo, Claressa Shields,
Serena Williams and Simone Biles. They earned their right to be
confident.

ELITE INSIGHT

Hannah White –
World Record Holder, Sailor, Broadcaster, Adventurer

I was twenty one when I did my first solo transatlantic race. I thought I knew everything, I thought I was absolutely indispensable, that I was just going to smash it. I really believed my own hype. The most interesting lesson I learnt from this was that I didn't actually make it to America! I had technical problems, had to retire from the race and come home, tail between legs, ego smashed to pieces. This was fundamentally the best lesson I've ever learnt in my life. I had far too much confidence, far too much belief in my hype. I was an awful lot better at painting a very very good picture of myself than I was at actually knuckling down and preparing for what I was about to embark on. Things won't be handed to you on a plate. You have to do the preparation; you have to be humble, no matter how good you think you are.

MOTIVATION

I think I was a naturally self-motivated person, my parents never pushed me, I asked them to take me everywhere, up and down the country for competitions. I was always pushing and wanted to do my hill runs on a Sunday morning and my extra weights sessions on a Monday night. The key for any young athlete is to maintain your own motivation levels if you want to fulfil your potential.

But how?

What motivates you is unique to you. You'll need to work out what this is and build on it. For me, it was always a strong desire to never let anyone down or disappoint them. My parents, my coaches, everyone who supported me had worked so hard to help me and I felt like the least I owed them was to consistently give it my absolute all.

I also found that a lot of my motivation came from success. I see an important distinction between a thought process that says "you need to be motivated to succeed" and one that says "success leads to motivation". Both have truth in them, but I found that a really good session in the gym made me feel great and made me want to do even better the next time. If I was lifting more, getting better training times or feeling fitter, I just wanted more, to push more and improve further and faster. I never wanted to plateau. If I reached a short-term training target, great, what's the next, tougher one? In skeleton I wanted to hit less walls, or hit them less hard! I wanted my times to get faster; I wanted to beat my competitors; I wanted to keep driving for more. It gave me constant feedback that I was doing better. I saw coaches seeing me get better; I rose up the rankings; I started showing I was more than just potential.

Every small success over the years led to more and more motivation to go beyond what I'd done previously. As the successes increased, so did my desire to outdo them.

Realising this and using it to my advantage was a big reason why I never ever lacked motivation.

TASK: Think really hard about what motivates you. Write down a list; save this list for when you are having a tough day and need that extra boost.

ELITE INSIGHT

Hannah White –
World Record Holder, Sailor, Broadcaster, Adventurer

It's incredibly hard to be out there day after day, being cold, alone, shattered, hungry, sleeping only twenty minutes at a time and thinking that I had to keep pushing and pushing myself. It's a constant race. I didn't have the option of just stopping working for an hour or relaxing. If I wasn't pushing, someone else will be. Maintaining my motivation was exhausting in itself. The driving force behind my motivation at times like that were the four hourly schedules, when we received updates on where the competitors were. I knew that the general public could also see these and I simply didn't want to disappoint people. There'd been an awful lot of people who'd rooted for me and who'd supported me. I wanted to do it for them. I found this my biggest motivator.

MY SUPERPOWER

To end this chapter, I wanted to tell you what I think my superpower was that drove me to fulfil my potential. What do you reckon it might be? Naturally thunderous thigh muscles? Freakish genetics built for insane speed and explosiveness? 20/20 vision that meant 90 mph on ice felt like a gentle stroll? The answer is none of those things. The answer is …

… self-awareness.

Through experience, I learnt what worked for me, what drove me, what motivated me, what gave me confidence, what maintained my well-being, how my thoughts affected my performance, what

I could do to improve all of these things. Being self-aware was a huge part of my success and was the main building block of one of the most important elements of all, my mindset.

Make it yours, too.

ATHLETE IN FOCUS

Sally Gunnell OBE DL –
Barcelona 1992 Olympic Champion; World, European, European indoor, Multiple Commonwealth Champion, 400-Metre Hurdles

I attributed as much as 70% of my achievements to my mindset. It's about knowing what you want to achieve, understanding what you need to do to achieve it, and executing it, believing you will win.

There will be down points, training sessions might not feel like they have gone well or similarly races too, but the key to having a winning mindset is to evaluate the negatives and turn them into lessons in order to achieve more in the future.

A winning mindset is a way of life, not something you try now and again, or when you think you need it. It needs to be woven into your life, a habit if you like, something that becomes natural.

Only you can be the best you can be. No one can do that for you. Believe!

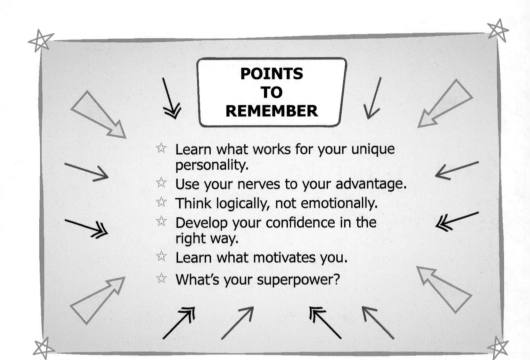

POINTS TO REMEMBER

☆ Learn what works for your unique personality.
☆ Use your nerves to your advantage.
☆ Think logically, not emotionally.
☆ Develop your confidence in the right way.
☆ Learn what motivates you.
☆ What's your superpower?

7 Training and Preparation

Training and preparation are everything if you want to succeed in sports. If you're well prepared and have done everything you can over the long term, then performance becomes all the more straightforward.

You already know this of course, but you'll also see an awful lot of athletes across all sports look back on their career, feeling like they could have improved it and achieved more. The purpose of this chapter is to equip you with the knowledge and tools to implement much of what's needed at an early stage.

The quicker you establish good habits, the better you'll be in the long run. You'll learn about planning, establishing habits, attention to detail and competition day preparation.

I'm proud to look back on my career and feel like, particularly after 2006 and the Turin disappointment, I couldn't have done anything else to work towards my goal. I was nicknamed "training champion" by my coach as I often performed better in training than I did in the early days of competing. It was only when I learnt to combine my training and preparation with everything else that came with experience (that hopefully you'll know after reading this book!) that I could genuinely say I achieved my potential. My hope is that you can do the same.

WHAT DOES ACHIEVEMENT MEAN TO YOU?

Every athlete has different goals that might change over time. Some, like me, aimed at Olympic gold, some aspire to be the greatest ever in their discipline, some want to represent their county or their country, some look towards the health and well-being benefits of sport and others look for pure enjoyment. Every one of these motivations is entirely positive and valid, the decision for you is to think about the levels of training and preparation that matches your aims and expectations.

Every piece of advice in this chapter can be applied at varying levels depending on your goals, but if your aspirations are towards the elite levels of competition then you'll need to understand that talent alone only gets you so far. There are so many highly talented athletes, but a much smaller amount of these are willing to make the most use of it through thorough training and preparation. More often than not, it's these that go right to the top.

Think really clearly about exactly what you'd like to achieve and then you can understand the levels to which you'd need to tailor your training and preparation.

There are so many factors that will affect you and your performance. Having a goal and a plan for every area will give you a clear list of areas you can start to improve – start finding those 1%s.

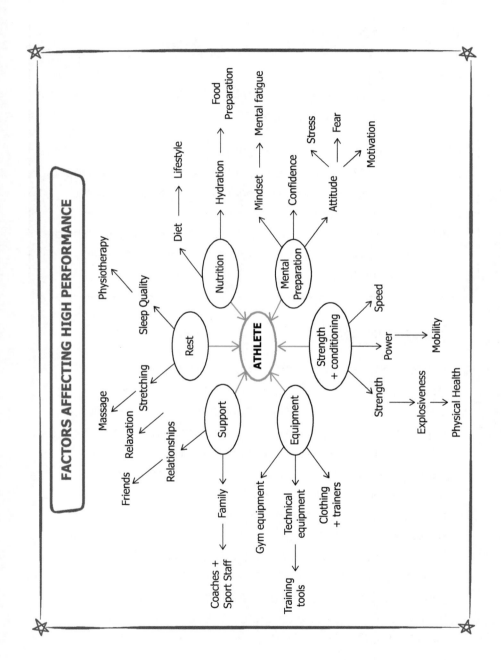

FACTORS AFFECTING HIGH PERFORMANCE

ELITE INSIGHT

Heather Fell –
2008 Beijing Olympic Silver Medallist, World and European
Champion, Modern Pentathlon

It's the work you do beforehand and the team that you build along
the way that will shape your future. I didn't realise this whilst at school,
struggling through day after day of endless hours in the swimming
pool, time in the gym and trying to squeeze a run into my lunch
break. So why did I spend more than 20 hours a week training so hard
throughout my teenage years? I loved what I did and I was addicted to
improving my performance.

HAVE A PLAN

Former world heavyweight boxing champion Mike Tyson once
famously said, "Everybody has a plan until they get punched in
the face". There's a lot to this quote, in some ways it shows the
importance of having a plan (although I'm not sure this was
Mike's intention when he was saying it!), as well as needing to
be flexible with the plan when circumstances change. This is
a great lesson to consider. Yes, you'll absolutely need to have a
training plan that you stick to and yes, you need to rehearse both
physically and mentally all the possible scenarios or events you'll
be competing in. Don't ever forget the importance of a plan B
(don't forget plans C, D and E as well!), though. This is part of
your overall strategy: what if things go wrong, the weather?
Injury? Train or bus was late? Your coach couldn't make it to the
event? You forgot something? There are hundreds of things
that can go wrong or situations that can change. When you're

designing a plan, make sure you factor in as many of these as you can so they're something you can just take in your stride when necessary.

ELITE INSIGHT

Colin Jackson CBE –
1988 Seoul Olympic Silver Medallist, World, European and Commonwealth Champion, 110-metre Hurdles

Getting to the top is never easy and if someone tells you there is a quick route, they are not telling you the truth.

Everyone who's reached their goals has always started by having fun and enjoying what they do. Whatever you do, put fun right at the top of the list.

Staying focused can be tough, but setting short-term targets can help; it means you can have the sense of achievement on a regular basis. This will lead to a feeling of well-being and encourage you to continue working hard. The formula is simple: Talent + continuous hard work + commitment = top performance.

Don't forget to learn from the best; take notes where you can and ask questions. Continuous hard work is not only physical!

Don't be too rigid with one plan without considering the need for it to change and *improve* at any stage. I think back to a push session I did many years ago and the notes I wrote in my psychology book. I wrote down that the whole session upset me massively. After my first push it went downhill from there and every push got me more upset. I could feel myself getting more frustrated and annoyed. I was conscious that I was slower than all the others, even though I felt really good sprinting and pushing the sled. It made me feel panicky, stressed and tense inside. I felt like I could just go outside and cry. In other words, it was affecting my training. Here's where my *plan* really worked. First, I said I'd always write notes on how training and competition felt (in this case, pretty rubbish). Then I'd *planned* to look at the negative sessions objectively and see what I could do to improve myself, rather than just worry about them. So I asked myself, "Would I have felt so bad and upset if I didn't see any of the other girls times?" Answer, no, definitely not. So what's the new plan starting tomorrow? Don't look or listen to the other girl's times. Sit on a chair out of the way. Listen to music after my pushes, don't look. Only think of myself and my goals. Be positive about *my performance*. Hey presto, it worked. The reason it worked is because I was learning what suited my training, planning accordingly, then implementing the (new and improved) plan.

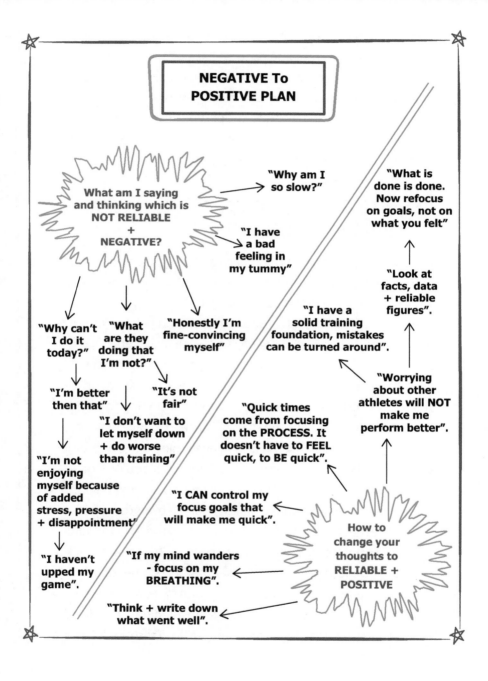

NEGATIVE To POSITIVE PLAN

What am I saying and thinking which is **NOT RELIABLE** + **NEGATIVE?**

"Why am I so slow?"

"I have a bad feeling in my tummy"

"Why can't I do it today?"

"What are they doing that I'm not?"

"Honestly I'm fine-convincing myself"

"I'm better then that"

"It's not fair"

"I don't want to let myself down + do worse than training"

"I'm not enjoying myself because of added stress, pressure + disappointment"

"I haven't upped my game".

"If my mind wanders - focus on my **BREATHING**".

"Think + write down what went well".

"I CAN control my focus goals that will make me quick".

"Quick times come from focusing on the **PROCESS**. It doesn't have to **FEEL** quick, to **BE** quick".

"I have a solid training foundation, mistakes can be turned around".

"Worrying about other athletes will **NOT** make me perform better".

"Look at facts, data + reliable figures".

"What is done is done. Now refocus on goals, not on what you felt"

How to change your thoughts to **RELIABLE** + **POSITIVE**

This goes for both yourself as an individual and for your wider team. All being on the same page is vital, but also ensure everyone has contingencies in place should they be needed. As we discussed in the teamwork chapter, trust in your team is so important. Your coaches and support bubble need just as much from you, as you do from them, create your strategic plan together, change it together when you need to.

GET INTO GOOD HABITS FOR TRAINING AND COMPETING

Plans are great, I hope this has been established, but they mean nothing unless they're implemented with absolute consistency. The only way to build this consistency (not just in sport, but in all aspects of your life) is to develop really good habits, from as early an age as possible. Every day you wake up, whether it's a training session or the day of a competition or match, you need to be prepared. Have everything ready to go, all set up for you to give you best performance. The simplest thing to begin with is to write a list of all the things you need to take with you. Prepare your kit, make sure you have everything and don't forget something vital for your sport. This isn't just your equipment or your clothing, it's your food, your water, your energy drinks, everything. When you write your list, visualise everything first, every aspect of the day, what will you need? Have you thought about the weather? Everything you'll need for travel? The quicker you develop these habits, the quicker they'll become routine and give you an advantage over those who don't prepare and don't have good habits. When they're panicking, running around and worrying about forgetting something, you'll be the one focussing solely on your event.

The following was my race day checklist:

☆ Preparation of the sled and kit the night before
☆ Sewing up my race bib
☆ Sled prep, runner polishing, taping
☆ Getting video notes from coach, changing any track notes
☆ Getting bag ready, kit bag and down bag
☆ Food and drink prep
☆ Track notes and book

☑ RACE DAY CHECK LIST ☑

CLOTHES

- [ ] Trainers
- [ ] Leggings
- [ ] Coat
- [ ] Gloves + Race Gloves
- [ ] Spare Socks
- [ ] Jumper

FOOD + DRINK

- [ ] Water
- [ ] Protein Powder
- [ ] Banana
- [ ] Electrolites drink
- [ ] Yoghurt
- [ ] Sandwich

TECHNICAL KIT

- [ ] Helmet
- [ ] Race Spikes
- [ ] ToolBox
- [ ] Sled
- [ ] Watch
- [ ] Race Bib + Safety Pins

EXTRAS

- [ ] Phone
- [ ] Money
- [ ] Spare Hair Tie
- [ ] Music/headphones
- [ ] Hot Water Bottle
- [ ] Book

MEDICAL

- [ ] Physio Tape
- [ ] Blister Pack
- [ ] Knee Support

✓ RACE DAY CHECK LIST ✓

CLOTHES

- ☐ ------------
- ☐ ------------
- ☐ ------------
- ☐ ------------
- ☐ ------------
- ☐ ------------

NUTRITION

- ☐ ------------
- ☐ ------------
- ☐ ------------
- ☐ ------------
- ☐ ------------
- ☐ ------------

TECHNICAL KIT

- ☐ ------------
- ☐ ------------
- ☐ ------------
- ☐ ------------
- ☐ ------------
- ☐ ------------

EXTRAS

- ☐ ------------
- ☐ ------------
- ☐ ------------
- ☐ ------------
- ☐ ------------
- ☐ ------------

MEDICAL

- ☐ ----------
- ☐ ----------
- ☐ ------------

ELITE INSIGHT

Hannah White –
World Record Holder, Sailor, Broadcaster, Adventurer

I concentrated a lot on looking after myself physically and mentally.
I made sure I was eating enough, sleeping enough and developing
knowledge of how my body worked. For transatlantic races I had to eat
freeze-dried food, I couldn't sleep more than twenty minutes at a time.
Yes, I needed to be strong to move the mast and such things, but I also
needed my brain to function fully and nutrition played a huge role in
this. I lost a stone and a half in three weeks during races so preparation
for this kind of extreme circumstance is essential.

No matter how many years I competed, I always checked
everything off on my list, without fail.

Habits don't just mean checklists though. It means everything
from arriving on time, never being late (building in contingency
to ensure this), cleaning up after yourself, never losing kit,
keeping equipment clean and tidy. I used to write down super
detailed notes, from waking up, leaving home, going to location,
setting up, warming up, waiting for the race, on the start line,
after the race, preparing for next run. The more my training
and preparation became ingrained through great habits, the
smoother everything went and the better athlete I became.

Start this process early; in fact, start right now.

TIME MANAGEMENT

What is your schedule for the day? Having a set routine and plan is super important. Preparation is key.

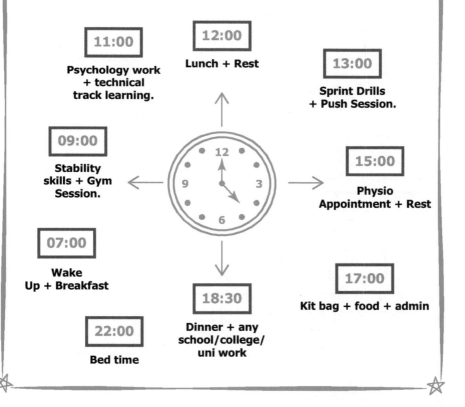

11:00

Psychology work
+ technical
track learning.

12:00

Lunch + Rest

13:00

Sprint Drills
+ Push Session.

09:00

Stability
skills + Gym
Session.

15:00

Physio
Appointment + Rest

07:00

Wake
Up + Breakfast

17:00

Kit bag + food + admin

22:00

Bed time

18:30

Dinner + any
school/college/
uni work

TIME MANAGEMENT

TASK

YOUR TURN →

Write out your
daily plan

ELITE INSIGHT

Rebecca Adlington OBE –
2008 Beijing Double Olympic Champion, World, European and
Commonwealth Champion, Swimming

My advice would be to always work on your relationship with your
coach. You want that communication, trust and respect as you develop
as an athlete. For me I loved training, I had to work on my nerves and
prep for racing. Keeping things simple, it wasn't life or death. I was
just putting my hat and goggles on going for a swim. I had to learn to
focus on the process and journey, not the outcome.

DETAIL

The higher the level of competition you're looking to achieve,
the smaller the margins between the competitors become. Think
about any sport at the elite level and it's incredibly rare you'll see
two top teams or individual competitors heavily dominate the
other. Major golf championships are usually won by just a couple
of shots, 100-metre races are often decided by one-tenth of a
second and many premier league football matches are won by
a single goal or end in a draw. This means that if your aspirations
are towards the higher end of sports, you'll need to make sure
you're squeezing every possible drop of performance inside of
you. The way you do this is by taking care of detail: every detail!

ELITE INSIGHT

Hannah White –
World Record Holder, Sailor, Broadcaster, Adventurer

In sailing we had to have a very close eye on what our competitors were doing during a race. Every four hours we'd get a tracker update with everybody's position, how they've gained time, how they've lost time, where they've moved to. There's a constant nervous anticipation of "has everyone just overtaken me and raced away?" This is especially difficult when you're in a light patch of wind, or you've had to stop to make repairs. I found myself with this slightly sick feeling that was constantly there. It's incredibly hard to manage this emotion when it's every four hours, constantly, for three weeks. There's no overnight parking; it's twenty-four hours a day, relentless pushing.

Think of every single detail of yourself as a sportsperson and as a person outside of sport. What could you improve? Or shall we rephrase that and ask, what can't you improve? I'd assume that the list of things that you can't possibly improve by even a fraction of a per cent is a very short list indeed. You most probably know that Usain Bolt is the world record holder over 100 metres. He did it in an almost unimaginable 9.58 seconds. Now watch the race on YouTube. You'll see that in the final few metres, Bolt turns his head to look at the time on the clock. Let's not get too picky about the greatest piece of sprinting by a male athlete in history, but that little glance may have cost him 100th of a second or more. It's an extreme example, but a good one to show that you can always improve what you're doing, no matter how insignificant the improvement might seem at the time and how good you already are.

This isn't about trying to lift just one more kilo on the barbell and end up injuring yourself, or doing more and more training until the stress on your body and mind become too much. It's about those *positive* improvements you can make. Can you train more effectively (rather than simply *more*)? Can you have better balance in your life? Can you ask more questions from more experienced people than you? Can you enhance your well-being? Can you learn to see the value of learning in losing (and indeed, winning)? Can you eat better? Sleep better? Do your job or your homework better? Be more organised? Can you not look left when you're running the fastest race in history?! I don't know if people will hate me for this line!!

ELITE INSIGHT

Jason Fox –
Former Special Forces Soldier, Television Presenter, Mental Health Advocate, Podcast Host

I put as much emphasis as I could into learning what I needed to learn to get a job done. I put a lot more effort into not necessarily being super fit, but being robust. It was much more about honing my skills like navigation and soldiering. You can equate that to whatever someone is trying to do, whether it's joining a rugby team where you need to make sure you understand the rules or to make sure you're on top of your game when it comes to passing or accuracy.

I never wanted to feel regret, so I was extremely detailed in my preparation. A few weeks before I knew I was heading out to the Olympics I started to do some research into my natural body clock and circadian rhythms. I found out that circadian rhythms are physical, mental and behavioural changes that follow a 24-hour cycle. They are natural processes that respond to light and dark and affect most living things (you can learn a lot about high performance when you look at animals and plants!). The most obvious example of a light-related circadian rhythm is sleeping at night and being awake during the day. The potential to impair your sleep, mood and cognitive performance is high and isn't good when you want to perform at your very best.

When you suffer jet lag due to travelling a long distance and passing through different time zones, your body's circadian rhythm gets affected due to the changes in the light-dark cycle. For me in 2010 flying from Britain to Vancouver in Canada, I "lost" 8 hours. My biological clock would have eventually reset, but it often takes a few days. I looked into how best I could offset the effects of jet lag and did as much research as I could. I found out that critically timed exposure to bright light and melatonin administration can help to reduce the symptoms. In the weeks prior to leaving for Vancouver I started shifting my daily habits by 30–60 minutes per day. I shifted when I ate, what time I worked out, when I went to bed, attempting to enhance day and night signals to the brain so I'd be performing at 100% as soon as I arrived there. I knew we were initially heading out to Lake Placid before the games, which was also a big help. We did a week of training there, before going off to Calgary for the second British holding camp. By the time we were there, I felt like my body clock was exactly where it should be so I never had to worry about jet lag at all when we headed to Vancouver. For those who might have flown straight into Vancouver from Europe (includes most other nations then), it would have been a far more difficult process and may have affected their performance.

Through a lot of research in the months and years prior to the Olympics, my team and I found that my peak natural testosterone levels were a few hours after I'd done a certain amount of specific weight lifting on a leg press exerciser. Sir Clive Woodward (known for his incredible attention to detail) who was the Chef De Mission at the time had a special leg press machine flown into Vancouver for me because there wasn't one available in the Olympic gym. I needed a specific one because of the issues with my discs and back which meant I couldn't squat heavy weights.

When I knew my race start time I could work back to when I needed to do the exercises and experience my natural peak. This would have had a tiny impact on my performance as it was the smallest amount of testosterone peaking, but when every 1% counts, I was going to do everything possible to improve my performance (in reality it had none because my start time was changed due to the race being delayed!) but it was symptomatic of the levels of detail we put into our preparation. It's also an example of taking personal responsibility in the sense that I spent a lot of time researching all of these theories myself and making sure I put everything into practice, to the letter. I was in the mindset of "why wouldn't I do it?" I was giving absolutely everything my best shot and leaving no stone unturned, it certainly couldn't have made my performance worse.

ATHLETE IN FOCUS

Dame Sarah Storey DBE –
Multiple Paralympic, World and European Champion;
Swimming and Cycling

There's a lot of talk about work hard and anything you want is possible, but rarely do people define that hard work. For me it is as much
about attention to detail as it is about being prepared to do more than
your opposition in terms of training hard. Being smart about how you
make improvements in your sport and knowing when to rest is as key
as dragging yourself out of bed on a cold winter day when you know
the weather is bad too. As an athlete gets older, teaching them how
to look in the mirror and make good decisions is a really hard thing to
do. It's a fine balance between doing enough, doing too much and
not doing enough. It's often referred to as balancing on the edge of a
cliff, the closer you are able to get the better your performance, but go
too far and you will fall off, get sick or injured and not compete well.
Not go close enough and you won't be as prepared as you should be.
For everyone that cliff edge is defined differently, each athlete is an
individual with physical and mental limitations that make them that
talent in the first place.

As a parent or coach finding an individuals' sweet-spot for working
hard, staying well and remaining confident and positive is so key. There
is so much truth in a mantra from the coach who I worked with in
the final half of my swimming career, "a happy athlete is a fast athlete".
Additionally, a piece of advice that stuck with me from the coach who I
worked with prior to my second games: "everyone can be ordinary, the
key is to be extra-ordinary".

The list of small improvements you can make is endless, but when you improve as many of these as you possibly can by just a tiny percentage, then you're well on your way to inching ahead of your competitors, because you understand the value of detail.

COMPETITION DAY

Training and competing are two very different beasts. It took me years to match my training performance to the actual days of competition. Once again, this came down to personal responsibility and attention to detail. There are no shortcuts to this, no one-size-fits-all solution to how you replicate your training performance into success in an event. Everyone is different and you'll need to find what makes you happy (remember, a happy athlete is a fast athlete!) and performing at your very best. See the value in learning from failure for this.

ELITE INSIGHT

Katy Livingston –
Olympian, World and European Champion, Modern Pentathlon

I was always aware that I performed much better with real nerves, the "feeling sick, tummy fluttering" type. At the Olympic Games in 2008, I hadn't performed well in the fencing event (usually a good one for me). Consequently, I was quite far down the results sheet after two events. The next event was the swimming, an event which was the least nerve-wracking to me. Knowing that I needed the nerves in my body to perform well, I popped my head out of the changing room before I raced to absorb the noise and feel of the crowd. Instant butterflies and I went on to swim a personal best. Next was the riding, an event which never failed to make me feel unbelievably sick with nerves (I had to get on a horse I had never ridden before and show jump over fences 1.2 m high). As I rode out into the packed stadium, I looked around at the crowd and took in the noise. I also thought of the millions of people watching from home on their TVs. I told myself "Do not embarrass yourself, Katy! Do not embarrass yourself!" I was the first non-pony club Pentathlete to compete at the Olympic Games. Instead of zoning out the crowd, I deliberately used them to increase the pressure on myself. My focus and determination became heightened and I rode a very good round taking down only one pole. It's important to identify what makes you perform well and use it to your advantage. And remember, it is different for each individual so do what works for you!

ELITE INSIGHT

Maria Costello MBE –
Preparing to Race the TT, All 37.73 Miles of Real Roads that Take You through Towns and Villages and across a Mountain

My ritual before I practice or race the TT course is not to be taken lightly. If you don't take the time to learn the course, that has over 200 corners, it can result in fatal consequences. I've been racing at the TT for over 20 years but my routine still includes watching onboard laps prior to heading out on to the course for real. More than that though is visualisation and this is vital for those times when the schedule is delayed and maybe you don't have access to your device.

My diet is tried and tested to avoid any unwelcome issues and fluid and essential amino acids intake is imperative as just one lap can take up to 19 minutes (hopefully less) and each race is at least 4 laps (and up to six) long.

The schedule at the TT is itself a force to be reckoned with as weather has a huge impact and being a tiny island in the Irish sea it is subjected to much change. So this part of the preparation is unique as you learn to control your bodies build up of adrenaline as the schedule is delayed hour by hour.

This is when knowing that you've already done everything in your routine up until this point – the delay – is paramount and gives you a "comfort blanket" type of feeling. When eventually the schedule is set and you maybe only have an hour for final prep, you already know you are ready.

If you didn't perform in a match or a race, don't worry, think about why? Be fiercely logical and learn invaluable lessons until you're at the point of knowing what works. This takes time. For me, it was all about feeling relaxed and not thinking about the other competitors.

When I felt my mind wandering, I noticed it and used breathing techniques to refocus. In fact, I found it so helpful that I wanted to finish this chapter with a detailed breathing exercise you can try from Lucy Stone.

Simple Breath Techniques/Mindfulness Exercises for Teens or Young People:

Lucy Stone, founder Meditation Rocks, Co-founder of The Hive Yoga Studio

How we breathe affects how we feel, and how we are feeling affects how we breathe.

Mindfulness is about trying to be in the moment, and not look-ing back or thinking too far ahead. Trying to focus on one thing at a time and being kind to ourself.

Stress isn't a bad thing; in fact we need it to keep ourselves safe from danger and harm, but sometimes the effects of stress can get in the way of what we are trying to do.

When we are under pressure, whether that is physical or mental stress, our brain automatically flicks our in-built fight or flight response switch which triggers a number of symptoms within the body; this includes sweaty palms, increased heart rate and faster breathing. But the good news is we can learn techniques to put the brakes on the fight and flight response, which means if we are feeling stressed, or anxious or our emotions feel overwhelming, we can start to feel a bit more in control.

Learning to breathe properly is like a superpower.

Learning to focus your mind and anchor it in the moment, without looking back or too far ahead into the future is a powerful weapon.

And here's how you can do it.

Take three deep breaths, in through your nose and out through your mouth.

As you breathe in, feel your chest expand so you can't squeeze any more air into the lungs.

Hold your breath and pause for a moment.

As you breathe out as slowly as you possibly can, let your muscles begin to soften and your body relax.

Do this three times.

MY TOP FIVE BREATHING AND MINDFULNESS EXERCISES TO HELP YOU THROUGH THE DAY

CALMING BREATH (COUNTING AND BALANCE)

If we want to calm the mind we need to breathe in and out through the nostrils.

Close your mouth when you are ready and start to breathe slowly in and out through your nose. We want the length of the inhale and exhale to be the same length, so you might like to count in for 1-2-3-4 as you breathe in, pause for a moment, and breathe out 4-3-2-1.

As you breathe out through the nose, listen to the sound the breathe makes, this breath is sometimes called the "ocean breath" as it sounds a bit like the waves, or the sea, so why not imagine you are sitting on your favourite beach as you do it.

FOCUS BREATH (NADI SHODHANA, ALTERNATE NOSTRIL BREATHING)

Sometimes our mind can be busy and whirling with thoughts, just at a time we need to be focussed and have a clear head. This is completely normal, and it is actually impossible to get rid of all our thoughts. What we can do is to try and focus the mind on just one thing, which should quieten the noise of everything else and make it easier to concentrate on what we want to do.

Nadi Shodhana is a technique which wakes up the mind and helps us to focus. With this exercise we are going to breathe through just one nostril at a time. It takes a bit of concentration which means it's tricky to think about anything else!

Take your right hand into the air and bring down your thumb and fourth and fifth finger leaving just your peace fingers. Pop your peace fingers onto the point on your forehead between your eyebrows, thumb on to your right nostril, and your fourth finger on your left nostril. Now close your mouth, release your thumb and breathe in as deeply as you can through the right nostril. Once you have breathed in as much as you can put the thumb on the nostril and hold your breath for a few moments, before releasing your fourth finger and breathe out fully through the left nostril. Now breathe in through the left nostril, when you can't breathe in anymore, seal the nostril with your finger, hold your breath for a few moments and then release the thumb and breathe out fully through the right nostril. That is one cycle.

You can do this as many times as you need to, but no more than ten minutes when you are just starting. Eventually, try and make the inhale, the hold, and the exhale to be of equal length if you can.

GROUNDING BREATH (USING OUR FINGERS TO BRING OURSELVES INTO THE MOMENT)

If you want to feel grounded in the moment, bring your thumb and first finger together in a mudra or circle shape. Take a few deep breaths in and out through the nose as you focus on the sensation in your fingertips. As you breathe out release your first finger from your thumb and relax your hand. As you breathe in again, bring your second finger to the thumb and focus on this sensation, and breathe out release the finger, relax the hand. You can work across to the little finger, and then back to the first finger. You might choose to bring in random fingers or more than one. For added mindfulness, you might count in your head, as you bring your fingers to your thumb. Aligning the breath and focussing on the sensation in the fingertips might help you to feel fully present.

ENERGISING BREATH (BELLY BREATHING)

When we breathe deeply and fully, it helps to balance the oxygen and carbon dioxide levels in our blood, this helps to feel more energised and alert. A good breath is like rocket fuel for the body and mind.

Quite often during the day, we can shallow breathe which means we are not making full use of our lung capacity and not getting the full benefit of the breath.

The diaphragm is a large muscle that sits at the base of the lungs. When we breathe in our gets smaller and moves downward, creating space for the lungs to expand and fill with air. When we breathe out, the diaphragm relaxes and moves upward, helping move air out of the lungs.

Diaphragmatic breathing or "belly breathing" uses the stomach, abdominal muscles, and diaphragm when breathing which helps get more air into the lungs.

Breathing from the diaphragm means we are really thinking about the quality of our breath. We can do this simply by placing one hand on your chest and the other hand on your belly. As you breathe in fully through your nose, feel your top hand and then bottom hand rise as the air fills your lungs. Hold the breath there for a moment as if you are holding an inflated balloon or beach ball, and breath out slowly through your mouth, with your lips in a circle shape so that you can tune in to the whooshing sound of the air leaving your lungs, try to relax as you exhale. Repeat.

HOW TO RELAX AND GO TO SLEEP (BODY SCAN)

We can you use our breath to relax our body and mind, before we head off to sleep, so this exercise might be good to do when you are in bed.

If you are comfortable, perhaps with your eyes closed, take a few deep breaths and feel the bed supporting your body. Let yourself relax as you breathe out.

Working your way up your body, from your toes and your feet, start to focus on the different parts of your body. As you breathe in, focus and notice any sensations or tension, and as you breathe out soften your muscles and relax. Travel all the way up the body from the toes to the head and face, relaxing as you go. Try and make your body feel lighter and more relaxed with every breath that you take.

BREATHING TECHNIQUES

Start at the bottom right of the square, + follow the arrows around the whole square to complete one deep breath.

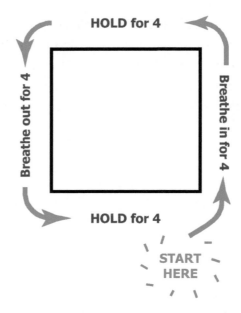

BREATHING TECHNIQUES

TASK To DO

Do this 3-10 times.
Relieves Stress + Tension.
CALMING.

- Feel your chest expand.
  In through nose.

- Pause for a moment and relax.

BREATHE in for 3

HOLD for 3

START HERE

BREATHE out for 3

- Breathe out as slowly as you can,
  let your muscles soften + body relax.

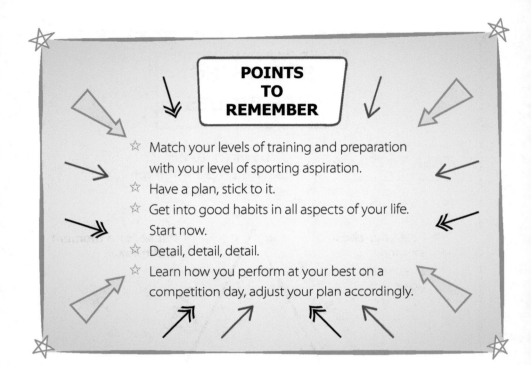

POINTS TO REMEMBER

☆ Match your levels of training and preparation with your level of sporting aspiration.
☆ Have a plan, stick to it.
☆ Get into good habits in all aspects of your life. Start now.
☆ Detail, detail, detail.
☆ Learn how you perform at your best on a competition day, adjust your plan accordingly.

8 Longevity

It's been many years since I retired as a competitive athlete, but those years of competing will always be something that stays with me and partly defines me. No matter the level you achieve, your sporting journey will always be part of your life. A lot of my friends and sporting peers who have left competitive sport have gone into PE teaching, working in sport or personal training as it's such an extension of who they are. The lessons you can learn from sport at any level can and will remain with you for your entire life. Your competing years are some of the most intense you'll ever experience, with all the highs and lows that go alongside them. But as every sportsperson knows, at some point you'll have to make the transition from being an athlete to being a "former" athlete. This isn't always easy, with many stories of struggle from those who miss the competing, the buzz, the training, the sense of achievement, the friends and teammates and the discipline (to name but a few). Athletes will often go to extraordinary lengths to prolong their careers. Trying to replicate the emotions of sport, the drive you had, the determination, motivation, pride you felt is difficult when you stop as an athlete; you lived and breathed your sport.

This chapter is about putting things in place to have as long and healthy a career as you possibly can, as well as preparing yourself for a life beyond your chosen sport. A long competitive career can be a wonderful thing, but not if it's at the expense of what you're able to do afterwards. Starting early with the right knowledge will go a long way to maximising your long-term performance and maximising your post-sport career.

> **THE PASSION AND MEMORIES OF YOUR SPORT WILL ALWAYS REMAIN WITH YOU. I CAN SHUT MY EYES AND STILL SEE MY FAVOURITE ICE TRACKS IN MY HEAD. I CAN HEAR THE NOISE OF THE SLED AND RUNNERS AS IT GRIPS THE ICE. I CAN SMELL THAT COLD, WATERY ICE, STILL REMEMBERING WHAT IT FEELS LIKE TO TOUCH. I CAN SENSE THE ATMOSPHERE ON COMPETITION DAY. THE FEELING OF PURE SPEED ON MY SLED.**

In the grand scheme of GB skeleton, I had a pretty good run of just over 10 years in the sport. In other countries, where the competitors tend to start much earlier, this is a relatively short time. In Germany, you'll see some 5-year olds practising skeleton in their school PE lessons! I consider myself fortunate to have had this amount of time, particularly when I think about the potential for injury, the competitiveness of GB selection and a whole lot of other factors.

TIMING

The unique aspect of GB skeleton is that athletes tend to come to the sport a little later than other sports, often from other events. We talent ID people, who are already well developed sprinters with measurable power and explosiveness as well as the maturity that comes with experience in other sports. We have seen so much success in skeleton because we have athletes with such a good grounding in other sports, without the wear and tear on the body that would have happened by specialising too early. My longevity came from having a really solid training background in all sports as I grew up and then from athletics. The lesson from this is not to concentrate solely on one sport from too young an age. Take your time, particularly in your early teens. Consider what early specialisation could do to your body in the longer term.

PRESSURE

In chapter 2 of the book, you'll have read all about the barriers facing young athletes and how you can overcome them. We spoke about things like distractions, being away from home, lack of equipment and others. What these can often lead to is athletes quitting their sports journey during those delicate teen years, only to try and pick it up again further down the line. While it can sometimes be a good thing to take a break from your sport, you'll also have to think about the importance of losing years of training and developing experience. It's far better to maintain training in your teens, while not putting too much pressure on yourself at such an early time. Remember why you took up the sport in the first place, ideally for all the enjoyment and fulfilment it brings. Having a long career in sport means holding on to motivation for the long term. Motivation is helped immeasurably by satisfaction in what you're doing. Try not to lose those important years by putting too much pressure on yourself solely to win. Winning is great, but it's also a short-term feeling. My focus throughout my career was never entirely on winning, but it was about getting the best out of myself in all areas. It was the enjoyment of training, and pushing my body, seeing how fast I could go, or how heavy a weight I could lift. The happy outcome of this was winning a gold medal, ironically.

By concentrating more on the process than the outcome, you'll put less immediate pressure on yourself and are less likely to quit and more likely to prolong your career.

FOCUS ON THE SMALL DAILY PROCESS GOALS, DO THESE CONSISTENTLY WELL OVER AND OVER AGAIN. TRUST THESE PROCESS GOALS AND THE RESULTS WILL HAPPEN.

MAINTAIN YOUR WELL-BEING

There's been a huge and justifiable increase in discussions regarding athlete well-being in recent times. In my years of competing it wasn't anything like as high on the agenda as it is now. The unfortunate truth is that we've seen sports careers cut shorter than they could have been and transitioning into a post-sports career being very difficult for some. Sport as a whole has learnt that looking after your well-being at all stages of your career is as important as your physical training. Every sport at elite levels now has their own athlete representatives and mechanisms in place with the aim of looking after and protecting their athletes. Many businesses are doing exactly the same, with a much greater emphasis on employee well-being. I often visit various businesses to deliver fitness, mobility or HIIT sessions and give talks on well-being and health, sharing the amazing things that sport can teach us. It's great that the conversations are being had and that we see so much more being done in this space, but make sure you take personal accountability for this as well.

Just because you're a talented athlete doesn't mean you're indestructible, either physically or mentally. There's been many examples of elite performers who from the outside looking in had everything while they conquered their sports. They had admiration, respect, financial benefits, glory and a place on a pedestal that seemed far removed from mere mortals. As we now know, in many cases this wasn't the reality behind the scenes. Never forget the importance of your overall well-being, both for the longevity of your career and for what you can do when your competing days are over. The earlier you can learn about the best ways to maintain and enhance your well-being the better. Seek out experts, learn what works for you, read books (I endorsed and fully recommend Dr Josephine Perry's book *I Can: The Teenage Athlete's Guide to Mental Fitness*). A few other of my favourite books when I was an athlete were *Achieving Excellence in High Performance Sport* by Tim Kyndt and Sarah Rowell and *Mind Games* by Jeff Grout and Sarah Perrin. Think about how you can take time for yourself, to recharge and reset and keep on top of this as much as you do other aspects of your performance. For a little added emphasis, I'll say it once more:

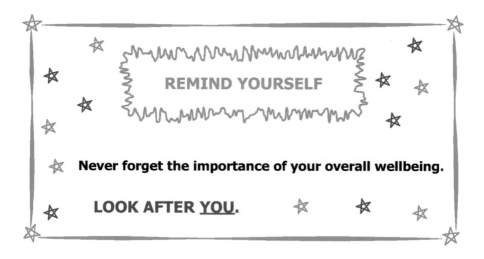

REMIND YOURSELF

Never forget the importance of your overall wellbeing.

LOOK AFTER <u>YOU</u>.

ELITE INSIGHT

Dame Sarah Storey DBE –
Multiple Paralympic, World and European Champion:
Swimming and Cycling

My parents were the driving force behind everything I did as a child and they remain a huge part of that force now. The key though is that they are behind me and not leading. From the very start of my career they made sure I was aware of the responsibility I have to myself to make decisions, to focus on my own performance and to follow a plan I am happy with myself. I think this has been one of the key reasons why I have enjoyed longevity in sport because I have always had that leadership role in my own career. My parents encouraged me to understand what I was doing and seek the answers if i wasn't sure and this has certainly helped me in my life outside of sport too.

TRUST THE EXPERTS

Let's start this section with a simple phrase: you don't know everything. Athletes have to concentrate on so many things during their career that they simply can't be experts on every single element of their sport or their performance. The good news is that there are plenty of people who *are* experts. Longevity means learning as much as you can from those who know more than you do. Read books, watch videos, seek information, talk to people and act on what they say. The internet is awash with both credible (and less so) information. Make a point of learning from those with credible experiences, whether that be through sports careers or academic qualifications. The more you can learn from physios, doctors, nutritionists, sport psychologists, coaches, former competitors and others, the better. Never stop asking, never get complacent and feel like you know it all, you don't. Longevity is helped an awful lot by your remaining humble about your levels of knowledge and maintaining a mantra of constant improvement and constant learning.

PREPARE YOURSELF FOR LIFE AFTER COMPETING

The longevity of your *sports career* shouldn't be seen as separate from the longevity of your *career*. It's sometimes easy to think that if you're a young athlete making great progress, showing big potential and conquering all that's in front of you, that you're all set for life. It can be a blessing and a curse that high achievement in sport can give you feelings of indestructability. It's great to be confident and have belief in yourself, but it's equally important to maintain that humility and work ethic when thinking about the long game of your working life.

ELITE INSIGHT

Vanessa Ruck –
"The Girl on a Bike", Motorbike Racer, Adventurer, Social Curator

The more serious end of injuries is when they can take away your sport altogether, as happened to me. I can tell you that this brutally hard. It may be a cliché, but I had to learn that one door closes and another opens, albeit it can and will take a long time to realise this. Take a step back and think about what tools you have. Which skills are still in your control? How can you shift and realign and take it to something in parallel to what you were able to do previously? You'll find that there are a lot of transferable things that you can apply in this situation.

Kite surfing was my main activity and to have this taken away was pretty horrific, I also have to accept that I'll never be able to run again. But there are many other things I can do with my time. I learned to think that running isn't the be all and end all of life. I can still ride a bike and there are people with worse injuries than me. For me it's a case of counting the blessings I do still have, for one thing, I could very easily have died. It took a serious amount of mental headspace to take a step back and think that even in the situation I'm in now, I'm lucky.

Injuries, whether serious or minor, can sometimes be the catalyst for even greater things. For me, *The Girl on a Bike* wouldn't exist if I hadn't been hit by that car. Sharing the battles that I was going through was something that resonated with a lot of people, as well as giving me the opportunity to connect with the world to some extent. If anyone had told me seven years ago that I'd ride motorbikes and connect with so many people on social media I'd have probably choked on my drink. I've learnt to relentlessly look for the positives in every possible situation.

The good news is that so many of the skills you've honed as an athlete are incredibly valuable in the working world outside of sport. Since retiring from competition, I've done a fair amount of work in the media and would have been lost without the tools I'd learnt from my competing days. Asking my ice coach for *feedback* on a sliding performance at St Moritz is for the same reason as asking Matthew Pinsent for his advice on presenting during an Olympic broadcast. Starting my very first ice camp in 2002 alongside people much better and more experienced than me was the same realisation that *humility and willingness to learn* are key when you're right back down at the bottom of the ladder again. Meticulous *preparation* on the intricacies of various ice tracks around the world in great detail and having to recall that information quickly while under pressure was pretty similar to presenting the gadget show! Standing at the top of Altenberg ice track and having to *breathe deeply* and *remain calm* when your mind is trying to tell you otherwise is pretty reflective of doing a live piece to camera. By being diligent about all of these things, you're not only helping your sporting performance in the short and long term but you're also learning hugely valuable skills for life after competing. I see so many examples of friends and peers of mine from various sports that have gone on to working for big banking firms in London because companies see the value in their lifetime of dedication, commitment and work ethic.

During my competition days I was aware they wouldn't last forever. I was also aware that sport was my passion and I'd love to stay in it for my whole working life. With this in mind I studied for a distance learning degree in sport performance. This wasn't easy so I needed a lot of discipline to make sure I completed it. Some athletes doing similar things would welcome the distraction of study from their day-to-day training. This wasn't the case with me. I really wanted to switch my brain off completely, watch a film or go for a coffee, but I knew I had to fight through these feelings. It was entirely worth it though and set me up well for the personal training and mentoring that I do now. Sport doesn't necessarily have to be the route you take either. I'd advise you to think about what your other passions might be and see if you can work them in parallel with your sporting journey with one eye on the future. You don't want to arrive at a very abrupt end point, whether through injury or anything else, having absolutely nothing to fall back on.

Sport is wonderful, yet unpredictable, sport is amazingly rewarding but can be unfair, sport teaches you fantastic life lessons, but you still need a longer-term plan.

Don't be fooled into thinking that elite sport will provide the life changing riches enjoyed by the world's best tennis players or golfers. These kinds of rewards are incredibly rare across the vast majority of sports. My motivation for skeleton was based around training, competing, friendships, achievements and experiences; it certainly wasn't motivated by money, which is why I always had one eye on a future outside of competing. I'd strongly suggest you do the same.

ELITE INSIGHT

Professor Greg Whyte OBE –
Professor of Sport and Exercise Science, Olympic Pentathlete, Author, TV Presenter, Public Speaker, Ultra-Endurance Runner

Competing at a time prior to National Lottery funding, when there was very little money in sport (there was even less in my sport, Modern Pentathlon!), I had a choice of studying or working. I chose to study completing my BSc in London, an MSc in the U.S.A., and PhD back in London, prior to retiring from international competition. Whilst I believe funding may have enhanced my performance (I won World Silver, European Bronze, and became and Olympian), I am grateful for the opportunity of creating a life beyond sport. Careers in sport are short, and I believe that preparing an exit strategy is crucial to ensure the quality of life you enjoy during your sporting career continues into mid- and later-life. I do not believe that creating a strategy detracts from the focus on performance. In contrast, I believe that a well-planned programme of activity alongside sport can have a positive impact on performance. This may, at times, add to the workload, however, I have long held the view that nothing good comes easy. That said, because I chose a subject I love, human performance (sport & exercise science), I have never seen it as work. Furthermore, studying the various disciplines of human performance (physiology, psychology, nutrition, biomechanics *etc.*) made me a better performer through a greater understanding of self. Combining my sport and academia, post-retirement, led to my appointment as the first Director of Research at the British Olympic Medical Centre, and Director of Science at the English Institute of Sport.

CONTROL THE CONTROLLABLES

It's that phrase again! You've seen it several times in the book far and you'll see it again. With everything in sport, there are things you can control and things you can't. The issue can be that many younger athletes don't yet have the necessary experience to realise just how many things you can control. On the one hand, this shows the importance of asking questions to those more experienced than you (a key controllable) and on the other, it's a reflection that many athletes look back on their careers with thoughts of "I wish I knew then what I know now". The whole purpose of this book is to give you the tools and information to minimise those regretful thoughts when your career is in its later stages.

Note to self

"Focus on what you can do well, not on what you can't".

For me, the penny dropped when I missed out on selection for the 2006 Turin Winter Olympics. To this point, had I *really* done everything I possibly could have to make those games? No. Had I *really* identified every possible controllable that I could maximise to make those games? No. Had I *really* ensured every decision I was making was geared towards getting the most out of myself to make those games? No. Was I enormously disappointed to miss out on those games? Yes. You can see the difference here. I considered myself to be a dedicated trainer; I worked hard, I didn't live a life of excess and I had pretty good discipline. But being pretty good is a world of difference to being elite. This goes for longevity, just as much as it does for winning a gold medal. Missing out on Turin was the kick up the backside I needed to realise that if I wanted to (a) fulfil my potential and (b) do it for the long term, then I'd need to reassess exactly what I meant by training and preparing well. I hope that after reading this you won't need to go through a disappointment like I did to realise this, but if you do, use it as fuel, like I did.

What characteristics can you think of that describe athletes like Sir Steve Redgrave, Dame Katherine Grainger, Sir Chris Hoy, James Milner, Christine Ohuruogu, Sir Ben Ainslie? All of whom had (or are still having) incredibly long careers in incredibly physically and mentally demanding events. The word that comes to mind for me is "discipline". Their careers went the way they did because they all learned from an early age that they need to look after every element of their lifestyle over a long period of time. They played the long game; they got into good habits early and carried them on throughout their sporting journey. Learn from them; there are far more stories of sportspeople who didn't do these things than did, and that's why these athletes are so rare and that's why they had so much success.

Think really carefully about what you can control, not just for the short term, the longer term is equally important. If you have a less-than-ideal nutrition plan in your teens, this will impact the longevity of your career. Look after your nutrition now. You need to eat well to rebuild those muscles, to minimise the risk of injury, to significantly improve your mental as well as physical performance.

You need to think about your energy needs for your sport, making sure you provide your body with adequate food/calories for your growth and development and making sure you have the right amount of energy expenditure for exercise and performance goals. The more you train, the more food you need, so you may need to change your eating patterns to reflect your daily exercise and the demands on your body. This may mean having larger meals and regular snacking to meet the increased energy demands on training days. Read up on this important area to gain knowledge; speak to your parents, guardians and coaches for support. Getting the correct nutrition is going to significantly affect your performance.

Make sure you're getting enough sleep. Just because you can function pretty well with the high metabolism of a teenager doesn't mean you're recovering properly, or your well-being is optimal, or your performance is as high as it could be. All of these are significantly impacted by the amount of quality sleep you're having. Getting into good habits from an early age is a fantastic controllable to work towards and something that will set you up for your full (longer!) career.

> **GOING TO BED AT THE SAME TIME EACH NIGHT, HAVING THOSE GOOD ROUTINES WILL SET YOU UP IN THE LONG TERM.**

Following Turin, if I (rarely) had money to spare, I'd pay for someone to come and do a massage. I needed to know that I was doing everything I possibly could to ensure my short- and long-term performance was being maximised. Massage helped me recover from and avoid injury and it became an essential part of my routine. That extra £40 for a massage that I didn't spend on drinking alcohol on a Friday night was one of a wide variety of small gains, that when all combined together made a huge difference to my longevity. I was investing in my body; I was investing in my future.

Post-2006, every decision I took had one thought behind it: "Will this help me make the next Winter Olympic Games?" All of these decisions became very black and white and boiled down to a simple yes or no. "Is it going to help?" "No?" then I won't do it. Four years is a long time in sport, but I knew I needed to start right there and then if my performance in 2010 was going to be where I wanted it to be. I had to be the very best version of me that I possibly could be, that's all I focussed on; the blinkers went on. It worked.

Take as much personal responsibility as you can, as early as you can. No one was telling me to have these extra massages. No one was telling me to be so cutthroat in my decision making for 4 years. No one was telling me to read more, ask more questions, learn constantly and do everything I could when no one was watching. You might very well make big strides during your training sessions when you're with your coaches and teammates, but what else are you doing when you're not with them? I can say for absolute certain that I wouldn't have experienced the feeling of standing on top of an Olympic podium had I not taken this conscious decision to look after every short- and long-term element of my sport. Instead, I'd be sat here now wishing I'd done things differently, because the opportunity was there.

The opportunity for a long career where you can fulfil your potential is there for you. Of course there's hardship, bad luck and adversity, but by controlling the controllables you'll find yourself with less things that can go wrong, less things that can cut your career short, less things that can affect your long-term performance and, most importantly, you'll have less regrets.

Get into the best possible habits now, in so far as you can; take your fate into your own hands. I promise this will never be something you'll regret.

ATHLETE IN FOCUS

Graham Bell –
5x Winter Olympian, Skiing, Television Presenter, Adventurer

Mulling over the idea of longevity, I've tried to break it down into the psychological, physical and technical aspects that would stand you in good stead as a young athlete. Probably the most important area to work on for a young athlete is your technical skills, whether you are playing football or alpine skiing having a sound base of technical skills is one thing that will set you apart from the opposition. However when you are growing up it is natural to want to compete, and basic drills can seem boring compared to the thrill of competition. The lesson is to never forget your technical skills, they make up the foundations from which you can build your sporting temple. Sport can be great for you physically, but in high level sport, that is not always the case, almost every athlete will have to struggle with injuries over their careers, no matter what the sport. The main lesson here for younger athletes is to learn to listen to your body and recognise the signals it is sending. Over training can cause chronic injuries, and racing back after a traumatic injury will often make things worse. Modern sports science certainly helps athletes judge their levels of fatigue, but do not make the mistake of become so blinkered by the will to succeed that you ignore the warning signs your body send you. Finally you are going to need drive and dedication to keep going and training hard through the good times and bad. For this everyone develops their own unique motivational tools, I personally used to harness any negative comments that were ever thrown my way, and use them to channel my fighting spirit. For example, I was once told by my ski serviceman, when I was struggling to come back from a knee injury: "I don't know why I bother waxing your skis, you only slow them down when you get going fast!" His words stung, but instead of punching him, I just swore to prove him wrong. Maybe I suffered from younger brother syndrome, but I was always quite fiery and aggressive as a youngster. Obviously this tool will not work for everyone, as we all have different personalities, the trick is to find the mental triggers that work for you.

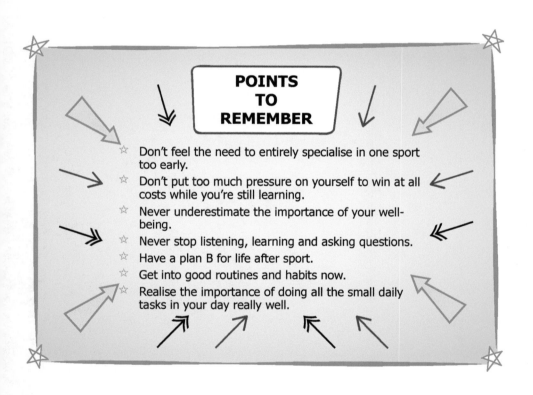

POINTS TO REMEMBER

- ☆ Don't feel the need to entirely specialise in one sport too early.
- ☆ Don't put too much pressure on yourself to win at all costs while you're still learning.
- ☆ Never underestimate the importance of your well-being.
- ☆ Never stop listening, learning and asking questions.
- ☆ Have a plan B for life after sport.
- ☆ Get into good routines and habits now.
- ☆ Realise the importance of doing all the small daily tasks in your day really well.

9 Dealing With Media and Attention

If you're a talented athlete and performing at a high level, then you'll start to get attention from the media. While this can be a really positive thing, there are also some potential drawbacks that I wanted you to be prepared for. This chapter is here to give you some advice on how you might deal with the increased attention, should it happen. Equally importantly, I wanted to emphasise how you can use the platform that sport can provide to achieve great things beyond yourself and into the wider community.

THINK LONG TERM

We discussed in the longevity chapter that it's never too early to start thinking about your post athletics career. This isn't just about your education (as important as this is) or your personal and professional development towards a longer-term career goal. It's also about ensuring you maintain and enhance your reputation and the perception of you from the outside while you're competing. Be aware that your behaviour during your career will be remembered. Following retirement from sports, you want to be respected, you want to know that the athlete you once were, was a role model, was positive and had all of those things that can help with a career afterwards.

Straight after winning the Olympics, I was offered a *very* significant sum of money to pose naked and spray-painted gold for the front cover of a national tabloid newspaper. Being a skeleton athlete doesn't bring with it the levels of financial fortune that being a premier league footballer or a top tennis player does. This meant that short-term cash windfalls were rare, which leads to them becoming tempting.

I took the long-term view though. What did I want to do following retirement from competing? What consequences would doing something like this have if I wanted to work for BBC Sport? Work with credible brands? Write a book …?

ELITE INSIGHT

Chris Price –
Head of Performance, English Institute of Sport

Really consider what you put on your social media, even as a young athlete anything you post may come back in the future.

Make your profile public and engage with your following, once you are 18 you can have a public profile which makes it easier to build your "brand".

When building your brand, be authentic and be yourself, if you want to work with other partners work with the ones you like and align too, it's all too easy to say yes to the first brand that wants to work with you, but in the long run authenticity will get you further.

In the same way as post-Turin in 2006 where all of my decisions were based on what would help towards my Olympic goal, my thoughts had turned towards what I needed to do *now* to help with a long-term career. I said no to that offer because I felt it would have negative consequences for what I wanted to do with my life, in exactly the same way I'd said no to so many alcoholic drinks, McDonalds or to skipping training sessions four years previously. I also thought my grandma wouldn't like it, so that sealed the deal!

You may or not be in the public eye right now for your sporting achievements, but if you are, or you are in the future, think carefully about the impact of your decisions and behaviour now. Are they helping towards your sports career or equally importantly, your post-sports career?

ELITE INSIGHT

Vanessa Ruck –
"The Girl on a Bike", Motorbike Racer, Adventurer, Social Curator

Your life as an athlete, because of the biology of the human body, has a time limit on it. If you've managed to build up a really strong social media base, it'll give you an easier foundation to then move on from being the active athlete, to being an inspirational former athlete. If you hadn't have done this and you've got an age where you can't compete anymore, things will be much more difficult in your post-sports career.

BE HONEST AND AUTHENTIC ON SOCIAL MEDIA

Sharing the aspects of your life that you're comfortable with on social media can be a really positive thing. People will follow you for different reasons, some because they admire your sporting talent, others because you're light-hearted, funny and serious and you give training tips or just have a cute animal in your house. Whatever the reasons, you'll often hear the term "authenticity" used as advice for using social media. I'd entirely recommend you be authentic, but really think about what this actually means.

ELITE INSIGHT

John Jackson –
Sochi 2014 Olympics Bronze Medallist, Bobsleigh

I have always been comfortable speaking to the media and never felt it affected my performance knowing I had to speak to them pre or post competition. My first World Cup race had camera crews moving around the start area, which took a bit of getting used to, but once I was comfortable with this, I used to get the camera person to pick up on our sponsors as part of the coverage.

I see speaking to the media as part of our role as an athlete, especially at the elite level, so enjoy and embrace the moment as much as you do competing. Always remain professional and polite and keep your answers measured, regardless of what emotional state you are in, depending on your result good or bad. If you need to take time to compose yourself, before you speak to the media then do so. I've had a mostly positive relationship with the media, but was always aware that anything I said could be misconstrued or used in a slightly different way that it was intended

ELITE INSIGHT

Hannah White –
World Record Holder, Sailor, Broadcaster, Adventurer:

People talk a lot about authenticity when it comes to social media. It's often a word that just gets banded about, then disregarded when they simply post their very best picture of themselves. I think the key is to paint yourself in exactly the same light as you actually appear in reality. That includes your weaknesses, your flaws. Clearly as an athlete you might not want your competitors to know your sporting weaknesses, but I believe there's very little to be gained in overhyping yourself. Enjoy the attention that's focussed on the success, rather than the attention that comes before the success has been achieved. Own and earn the attention, rather than create it.

Life isn't always glamorous and people know this. If you want to use your platform to be a role model and sport can certainly give you that platform, then be a real one. No-one expects you to have a perfect life and it can be just as inspiring to see those in the public eye having the same day-to-day challenges as everyone else. Professional athletes are perfectly normal people and they have good and bad days just like their followers. Yes, it's nice to see sunny training pictures, winning races or scoring goals. But it's equally good to see some "normality" and some of the less shiny side of a sports person's life.

I'm conscious of this in my own feeds where it's fun to post about training, exciting experiences or some throwback shots of my competing days. You'll also see posts about normal daily things like crazy kids, a crazy cat or when irritable bowel syndrome makes me bloated and feeling rubbish (glamorous, hey?). I want my feed to be *authentic* because it's a truthful way of connecting with followers. You can make a positive impact through honesty, instead of attempting to show a lifestyle that's unattainable (for you or your followers).

ELITE INSIGHT

Vanessa Ruck –
"The Girl on a Bike", Motorbike Racer, Adventurer,
Social Curator

I know that there are a lot of other female bikers who get a *lot* of nasty comments on social media. I go with the approach that I'm going to be entirely real with my posts. I'm honest, I'm open, I try to be entirely credible, I'll never try to be anything I'm not, I don't pretend to have the answers to everything, it's just me and my opinions. I think that when I put myself out there on social media in such an honest way, it's that much more difficult for people to throw stones at.

Be true to who you are, don't think about your social media being entirely about *you.* But think about how your story and your experiences can be relatable to someone else. What can you do to inspire other people, to help them in their day? Could they get up in the morning and give the sport you're doing to a high level a go? The engagement levels in your posts will be so much higher if you're giving. Don't try to make it entirely *me me me.*

BE A ROLE MODEL

Sport teaches you an awful lot. The higher your achievements in it, the more you learn and the more experiences and knowledge you have to pass on. This is where sport can be an incredible force for good in the community as a whole. Former athletes from any sport will often have built-up significant platforms on social media and they can be used to do an awful lot of good. The recent pandemic has brought this into such sharp focus in so many ways. Want to see how someone can overcome adversity in their training? Watch Holly Bradshaw create a pole vault weight with a tin of beans. Want to see how a socially conscious athlete can directly impact government policy? Watch how Marcus Rashford successfully campaigned for free school meals to those children that needed it most. Want to see how to exercise or eat correctly from those that have spent a lifetime doing this? Take a look at the social media feeds of many former athletes who are committed to sharing everything they know (including mine, it's great I promise!).

In the spirit of humility, I'll take myself out of the above list of athletes and say that a big part of the reason Holly Bradshaw or Marcus Rashford could make a positive impact on people was down to them being at the top of their sport. This can be a little-added motivation for you to make it in your sport. The higher you go, the bigger your platform and the greater the positive impact you can make.

If you're a talented athlete with aspirations of making it to the elite levels, you can use that platform that comes with it for so much good. Think about this when you're posting on social media or you're behaving in the "real world". You might find yourself with a unique ability to positively affect the lives of a lot of people who'd look to you for advice or motivation. The world has plenty of negativity, but you can use your platform for positivity, you can be a force for good, you can be a *role model*.

ADVERTISING

Success in sports will attract attention. Companies and organisations will notice this attention and will in many cases want to be associated with it. Most sports don't come with huge pay cheques, so sponsorship can be an important part of your ability to generate an income.

The likelihood of companies being interested in you is of course initially developed via your sporting success. Leaving this aside (although it can be a little extra motivation to train correctly), you should also be thinking about why else you'd be a good option for a company to work with.

ELITE INSIGHT

Chris Price –
Head of Performance, English Institute of Sport

Make sure you follow the guidelines set by your National Governing Body when using social media, particularly if you are in their kit/national kit. If you are ever unsure always ask.

If you do brand partnerships both paid and free, or you are sent free products which you put on any social media, make sure you follow the advertising rules and list it as "PR product", "Ad" or "partnership", this will keep you out of trouble with expensive fines.

Most importantly, just be yourself and do not worry how long it takes to build your following up … it takes time!

Put yourself in the position of someone looking for athletes to endorse their product, what would they look for? More importantly, who would they like their product to be *associated* with? This is a big decision for an organisation to make. Their brand perception is everything, so they'd most likely avoid any athlete that wouldn't put their product or company in the best light.

Everything we've discussed so far in the chapter around behaviour, positivity, being a role model and being authentic are all entirely relevant for what a company may look for. If you don't behave as you should, you're seen as inauthentic or you don't act as a role model should, then your sponsorship and advertising potential is lowered.

Authenticity also goes for the products you actually advertise. I have a very firm rule that the companies or products I work with would only be those I'd honestly recommend. I simply couldn't tell my followers to buy something if I didn't feel like it was a genuinely good and positive thing.

Think carefully about the long-term perception of you as a person that would come with which products or services you worked alongside. Short-term money may not be the best option for your long-term career (remember me and the gold paint!).

ELITE INSIGHT

Vanessa Ruck –
"The Girl on a Bike", Motorbike Racer, Adventurer,
Social Curator

Sponsorship is key to the success of athletes in many (most) sports. With this in mind, social media is incredibly important. You simply can't get the same levels of sponsorship without it.

Just being on the podium is no longer enough.

In the industries I've had contact with, if you can get your message out to people, on top of the fact that you're on the podium, or you're getting other publications talking about you, then you've got a hell of a lot more chance of brands wanting to work with you. A really extreme example of this is me! I've never been on the podium, but I'm sponsored by the likes of Michelin tyres. This is because I can get the message out in an engaging, authentic, credible way for people who would potentially buy Michelin. That's not say I won't be on the podium, one day …!

I'd advise against overly shouty brand marketing. Yes, work with brands, put out brands that you trust and that you'd spend your own money on. As soon as you become just a mini advertising channel, you'll shut off your followers who'll lose interest and disengage. If you recommend something, make sure you really *do* recommend it.

Think about your relationship with your followers in the long-term over shorter-term payments for things you might not really believe in. If you focus on this, the payments will come further down the line and your brand will be far more powerful.

DON'T BE AFRAID TO SAY NO

More often than not, you won't be in control of the questions you'll be asked from the media. This isn't something to be afraid of, but there's always a possibility that you'll be asked about things that you either might not have a lot of knowledge about or simply don't feel comfortable answering. There's absolutely nothing wrong with being honest and saying, "I don't really want to talk about that" or "I'm not comfortable discussing that". The choice is always yours, so only answer the questions that you want to. If you don't have knowledge of a certain subject you'll look far worse if you just winged it and try to say something that might not be correct.

ELITE INSIGHT

Vanessa Ruck –
"The Girl on a Bike", Motorbike Racer,
Adventurer, Social Curator

I take a different approach to each different platform.

I tend to post similar things across the different platforms, albeit with some definite variations. There are things I'd post on LinkedIn that I wouldn't post on Facebook or Instagram. But anything that goes on Instagram can generally go on LinkedIn.

I use LinkedIn as a professional networking environment. I'd be communicating with brands I work with, or getting myself on the radar of brands I'd like to work with.

Facebook tends to be a lot more conversational, people tend to comment more, become more engaged. I find multiple photos on a Facebook post work really well.

I personally avoid political discussion on my social media, largely as there are so many viewpoints from followers that may or may not share my views or vice versa. My brand is largely about my recovery, bikes and bike riding and I'm fully aware that my followers are looking for content about those things, not about my political views.

YouTube can be great, but also really hard work. You'd need to do a lot of videos, consistently and keep it going in the long term. Until you can really put the time into it to do it well, then think carefully about using it. Unless you can pay someone to edit your videos, the workload can get out of hand. If I take a typical day of riding motorbikes, I'll have 40 gigs of content that I've then got to work through.

Social media platforms thrive on data that data comes from people using and engaging with their site. Anything you can do to bring people on to that platform is great news for them, so you'll end up in a more favourable position with them and their data analytics.

I was once asked questions about certain political circumstances potentially leading to activism or boycotts of a sporting event. I didn't feel like I knew enough about the situation and especially when the issues can be sensitive, I just preferred not to answer. If someone wanted to ask me about my training, or the nuances of tackling a particular corner at Altenberg ice track, then great, fire away and I'll tell you everything. But if it's something outside of my knowledge base, then I'd much rather not speak on something I don't fully understand.

Never be afraid to say no to discussing things you don't want to.

ELITE INSIGHT

Ellie Simmonds OBE –
Multiple Paralympic Champion, Beijing 2008, London 2012, Rio 2016 Swimming:

I think media can be both a positive and a negative in sport. A positive in that you can use your platform and the opportunities it gives you being in the media. It can also drag you down when you receive negative media when a race/competition doesn't go well. I find a big tip for me is creating that barrier, creating that chance to step away especially during big blocks of training and competitions coming off social media and not going on the news! If you see one negative comment it can really drag you down, and that doesn't bode well for when you're about to compete in the biggest race of your life.

Take the realistic view that everyone has their opinions, but if you're happy and the people you love are happy, then that circle you're in will be positive.

I think sport is a huge mental game, you can be physically in the best shape of your life but if you're mentally struggling or not happy/confident it can be a real game changer. I think for me I just try to focus on the things I can control. Yes there are times where I've been down due to the media but I try to think realistically and talk about how I am with other people.

Talking to others in the same boat or out of the picture of sport can really help put a perspective on life. As athletes we can be so blinkered with things like that, we don't realise why we do the sport and the huge positives we get from it.

Similarly, be aware that you might be asked an extra question at the end of an interview when you might have let your guard down a little. Even if the recorder has been switched off and the atmosphere is more relaxed, don't say anything you might later regret. The vast majority of journalists are fantastic and they have no agenda to put you in a negative light, but there's always the possibility that one might be looking to stir up some controversy.

ELITE INSIGHT

Chris Price –
Head of Performance, English Institute of Sport

Most journalists are good people who want to showcase your achievements, but some just want a story which makes headlines. Both have their place but it can be difficult to manage.

If you are in a sport where you're fortunate enough to have someone with communications experience, reach out to them and ask advice; they will always be happy to help.

Remember, anything you say to a journalist from the moment you walk into a room to the end of the meeting could be used; there is no such thing as "off the record".

Practise makes interviews easier so the more you do hopefully the more comfortable you will become, no one becomes an expert overnight, so if a local paper asks to do an interview, say yes; it's great practise.

If you do not know the answer or maybe you do not feel comfortable answering a question, just say you would rather not answer. Journalists should respect that response.

Once again just be yourself; do not try to be someone else or mimic someone else because it is so much harder to maintain this. Authenticity will shine through every time.

The final test I always ask myself or get people to ask themselves whether on social media, in interview or in the press is, "If I saw that on the front page of the *Daily Mail* would I be happy and how would my friends and family react?" If you think you would be unhappy then don't post it or say it!

I've had it several times when someone has just fired one more question to me. However small your comment might be, it can be the headline the next day! These questions are normally nothing to do with your performance or the interview, so while you should be yourself as much as possible; have a slight guard up against such situations.

ELITE INSIGHT

Vassos Alexander
Sports Presenter, Virgin Radio, Author

Don't fear the media, they can do a lot of good, but always have your wits about you. The main reason (credible) journalists want to interview you is because you're good at your sport. They want to speak to you because you've just achieved something really impressive. Try not to be too guarded (within reason), don't overthink it and just be yourself.

Always be honest, don't be scared, enjoy the interview and see it for what it is, a celebration of your success.

Dealing with Negative Questions

Be clear about the things that you'd prefer not to talk about. I remember speaking to a leading sportsperson several years ago whose mother had recently spent time in prison. They'd just achieved something exceptional and another reporter asked them about their mum. The athlete in question simply and politely said that they weren't here to talk about that, but feel free to ask them anything else. It was perfectly handled by them and you should always feel entirely free to say something similar.

In another situation I was about to talk to an athlete, who, again, had just produced an exceptional performance. They'd just come from a really difficult (and overly personal) interview that I'd overheard. They'd really grilled her and she was a little shaken up and understandably guarded when it was my turn. I wanted her to be comfortable so the first thing I said was "I hope you don't mind me saying this, but we absolutely love you, massive congratulations on your performance". Essentially, I wanted her to know that all the press aren't out to pick away at sportspeople and most of us simply want to discuss their performance. Around a week later, she contacted me to thank me for those words, which was lovely of her to do so.

Finally

Be happy to speak about yourself. You've worked extremely hard to get to the stage where the media are keen to talk to you. Try and see it as a positive experience. Congrats!

ELITE INSIGHT

Eleanor Oldroyd –
BBC Sports Reporter

In my experience, most sports journalists are sports fans; we want to see you do well and celebrate your success! Our job is to help our readers, viewers and listeners get to know you so they are invested in your achievements.

If you're doing interviews ahead of competition, think about interesting or even quirky things to tell us about yourself; maybe you have a dog who goes on training runs with you, maybe you bake cakes to relax. A good journalist will probably have checked out your social media so they may pick up on stuff you post. But it's your choice what to share and what you'd rather keep private.

If everything goes to plan, then everyone will want to hear your story, and it can be a bit overwhelming. One of my best memories at the Olympics was interviewing Amy after she won her gold medal in Vancouver. We were staying in a lovely chalet in the centre of Whistler so we invited Amy to come and sit on our sofa to be interviewed for BBC Radio 5 Live. She'd already done loads of interviews that day so we tempted her by saying we had English tea and we'd bought special biscuits!

It's much harder to interview athletes when things haven't gone well. It can be brutal to see someone who you want to see fulfil their potential having to walk through the mixed zone – the area where journalists and broadcast crews gather to get quotes immediately after competition – when you know it's the last place in the world they want to be. On more than one occasion I've just wanted to give them a hug. In those situations, though, remember that the journalist is just doing their job and they're really not trying to catch you out. We're a friendly bunch generally, and we're in the business because we love sport – just like you do.

I retired in the middle of 2016 from the sport of bobsleigh, but felt like I'd never been able to fully walk away. Becoming an Olympic Medallist and the presentation of the medal, allowed me to close that chapter of my life.

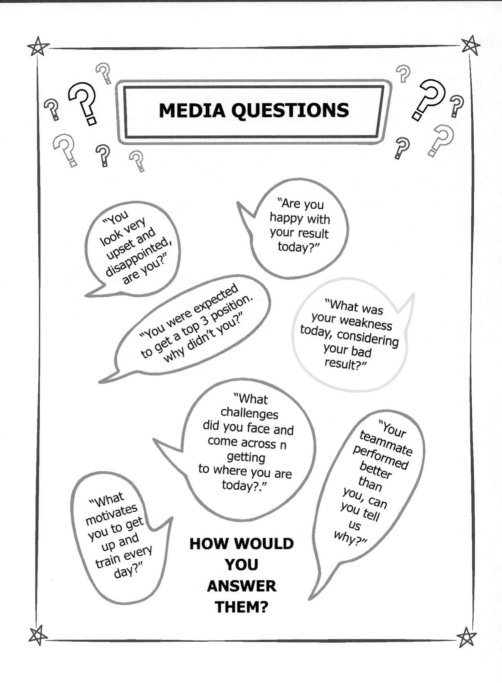

KEEP A BALANCED PERSPECTIVE

Receiving recognition from the media about your sporting achievements can be a great feeling. People noticing your success can feel like reward for all of the hard work you've been doing. That's all fine, but try to remain level-headed, despite the praise. If your profile is building, then remember what's building it. There's always someone else out there who'd love to take your place and will be working hard to do this. If you take your foot off the gas and think you're just more talented (because the media says so) then you'll be in for a shock when your performances start dipping.

ELITE INSIGHT

Hannah White –
World Record Holder, Sailor, Broadcaster, Adventurer

The reality is that having a profile helps. I'd never shy away from this (I now work in TV!) but it has to come hand in hand with you doing the hard graft, the work and the preparation. Without this graft and preparation, there's no point in having a media profile. On the flipside, if you *do* all of this work and you don't have a media profile, then it's a bit of a waste. It's a tough world out there with sponsorship, endorsements and everything else that comes with those, but you have to make sure you're performing at a high level first.

Use external praise as a motivator to say to yourself, "if they think I'm good now, just wait and see what I'll achieve in the future because of my work ethic". There are far too many stories of sports people being built up into being the next big thing, only for them to believe this and start coasting. Keep your end goals at the forefront of your mind. If you break world records, win world cups or grand slam tennis matches, then fantastic, enjoy the praise, but until you've done that, keep working towards them no matter what people are saying about you.

ELITE INSIGHT

Hannah White –
World Record Holder, Sailor, Broadcaster, Adventurer

The media side of my career was absolutely licked, it was excellent, but my practical training side of things, really fell by the wayside. I'd be talking to the media and saying "yes I'm the next big thing", and in turn they'd write that I was the next big thing, then I'd read it and think "wow, I really am the next big thing". Before you know it, you almost feel like you don't have to try, you don't have to prepare, because you believe what people have written about you. It's a really dangerous cycle that you can get yourself into. Suddenly you can then find yourself in the middle of the Atlantic, failing a race and having to turn home and sail back. All those people that were quick to say that I was the next big thing are suddenly going to turn into critics. That was really hard to deal with. I was going from winning races and doing well to suddenly lots of people saying I was too young, too inexperienced, that I was never going to make it.

It did mean that the next time around, I focussed very little on the media or my profile and I concentrated entirely on doing well for the race. I'd say there's more of a happy medium to be had here, but I can tell you that the second way of doing it was far less risky!

FINAL THOUGHTS

Like much of your sporting journey, dealing with the media and increased attention can have high points and low points. While writing this chapter, there's been a lot of coverage around tennis player Naomi Osaka withdrawing from the French Open. Naomi announced prior to the tournament that she won't be doing any media interviews due to effect they have on her mental health. She subsequently withdrew entirely from the championships, with part of her statement reading:

"The truth is I have suffered long bouts of depression since the US Open in 2018 and I have had a really hard time coping with that."

"Anyone that knows me knows I am introverted, and anyone that has seen me at tournaments will notice that I'm often wearing headphones as that helps dull my social anxiety."

"Though the tennis press has always been kind to me (and I wanna apologize to all the cool journalists who I may have hurt), I am not a natural public speaker and get huge waves of anxiety before I speak to the world's media."

"I get really nervous and find it stressful to always try to engage and give you the best answers I can."

The first point I'd make here is that Naomi did exactly the right thing for her. Priority number one for anyone involved in sport (or anything else) is to look after their well-being. If dealing with the media is having a negative effect to the point where your mental health or well-being is being affected, then you should be brave and confident enough to simply say no. Even the world's finest athletes can find it difficult to deal with the attention; and they, like you, should only do whatever you're comfortable with.

If you find yourself in a position where you're getting a lot of attention and media interest, then seek advice from those who've been there before you. It may be a good idea to do some basic media training and make sure you ease yourself into it. I certainly wasn't confident in front of the cameras until I'd built up several years of experience with it. Go easy on yourself, take things slowly and enjoy the positive side of it when it happens. Very much like your sports journey!

ELITE INSIGHT

Lewis Moody MBE –
World Cup Winner, Rugby Union, England

From my experience, dealing with the media was a rollercoaster of highs and lows. From World Cup glory to World Cup ridicule.

During both, when dealing with the media I always felt I was on guard, careful not to have my words taken out of context and not wanting to negatively impact myself or the team. I was hoping to control the headlines or what was written.

This was madness of course as whatever I said or did could be taken whichever way they wanted to fit the narrative they or their boss was working to. I often felt frustrated and angry that my words had been misconstrued or used out of context.

So to work with the media, I needed to understand myself better, that being myself was enough, that we can't be perfect, that people see through the mask we put up. I learned not to seek affirmation from external sources like the media to determine or confirm how well I had played. I would also then look for this affirmation when I had not played so well, which was only ever going to have a negative impact on me mentally.

Over time I came to realise you cannot control what is said about you, so don't try. Know everyone will have an opinion on you the individual and you the player and some people may mix the two. But understand they don't know you the person, they are judging you on what they see you do as an athlete. They are not judging you as a person.

Be okay that sometimes you may not agree with what they say, sometimes they may say something that isn't true.

This is okay because ultimately the only opinions I really needed to hear were those that mattered to me. Mine, my teammates, coaches and family.

If I could go back and offer myself any advice on working with the media, I would say "don't put so much pressure on yourself, be you, be open and honest in success or failure. Support those around you, celebrate their success and if you are to be critical, be critical of yourself.

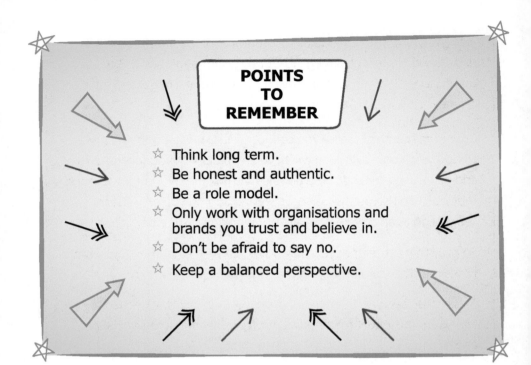

POINTS TO REMEMBER

☆ Think long term.
☆ Be honest and authentic.
☆ Be a role model.
☆ Only work with organisations and brands you trust and believe in.
☆ Don't be afraid to say no.
☆ Keep a balanced perspective.

10 Success and Peak Performance

First of all, a big well done on reaching the final chapter. My hope is that you've learnt some valuable lessons that can stand you in good stead for your sporting dreams, whatever they might be.

I wanted to use this last chapter to take you through the experience of being in that moment that you've always worked toward; for me, it was the Olympic final. Most importantly, I want to outline how the lessons you've hopefully learnt through reading the book were so vital to me during those crazy days in February 2010. You'll see how so many of them *directly* resulted in me achieving my lifelong goal and how without them I wouldn't have stood a chance.

THE BUILD-UP TO THE FINAL RUN

Racing at the Olympics is over four runs across two days. Day one starting order is based on your world ranking at the time. This made me start number five. For the final run, the order goes from the slowest slider to the fastest from the previous three runs. It also determines the intensity of pressure you'll be feeling. A slow first three runs might bring a sense of disappointment knowing you're most likely out of contention. A quick first three can mean on the one hand elation that you're right up there, alongside an even greater sense of pressure to deal with. I went into the final run ranked number one. I was the last one left in the changing room, everyone else had left and were at the bottom of the track, having completed all four of their runs. It was just me alone standing on the start line. Knowing I was in the lead, in first place, but I still had that fourth and final run to do. It mattered. I couldn't make a mistake.

My whole life, everything I'd worked for, all those early mornings with my parents driving me all over the place, every training session, every decision I'd ever made, every piece of learning I'd ever done all came down to one run lasting around 54 seconds.

I knew myself as an athlete, I knew what worked for me and I knew what didn't. So what did I do prior to the run? The answer is exactly the same as I did before any run based on what I'd learnt. I took myself away from everyone else. I went upstairs in the changing room, and found a quiet, smaller place where all the physio beds were. I sat in the corner by the window that was taped over with union jack flags so I couldn't see anything happening outside. I could hear the buzz, but had no idea what was happening and I liked it this way. In my mind, I just pretended it was a normal training session. I convinced myself that it wasn't an Olympic race, that everything I'd ever worked for wasn't just about to come down to this one run.

I knew that I only ever performed well when I was calm, relaxed and happy. I was so often better in training than I was in competition, so it was time to tell my brain that it was just that, a good old training session. It was a deliberately relaxed environment in that room, clearly a fake relax, but much preferable for me than to be downstairs in the main changing room. On the final run of an event, the changing room gradually gets emptier and emptier as each competitor goes outside to complete their run. That in itself intensifies the feeling of tension as slowly but surely the amount of people in there gets smaller and smaller and the room becomes quieter and quieter. Knowing that I was the very last athlete to go would have meant staying for the full duration, which was almost an hour. Feeling gradually more tensed, gradually less relaxed. Knowing my optimal routine as I did, that was about the worst possible environment for me to be in, so away I went.

ATHLETE IN FOCUS

Susie Rodgers MBE –
2012 London Paralympic ×3 Bronze Medallist, 2016 Rio de Janeiro Paralympic Gold and ×2 Bronze, Multiple World Championship Medallist, Swimming

When I won gold in the 50 m butterfly event (S7 class) in Rio 2016, if you have seen the footage which is now quite famous, I was more than a little shocked! I remember thinking winning silver was a possible outcome, I was very excited about that, but trying to keep calm. One of the British coaches I was working with gave me a helpful pep talk as I walked to the call-up room prior to my race, it was designed to get me feeling I could win, but I only realised this afterwards. I don't think anyone on the team, least of all me, expected me to actually win the race. It isn't to say they were thinking I wasn't good enough, but we were all realistic about what I was up against. However, it just went well from start to finish. I felt a sense of calm about the outcome, I had prepared for any eventuality mentally and had visualised all those outcomes privately, rehearsing my emotional reaction to each. The one I didn't dwell on was winning! I just went out thinking, "You are a performer; give this crowd something to cheer about". I really just saw myself going through the motions and executing what I had rehearsed many times in training. Nothing can prepare you for that moment though. I touched in and there are lights that flash on the blocks as you hit the wall, one red light for a win, two for silver, three for bronze. It was a 50 m race, so the board with the results was behind me. I was exhausted, as you always are at the end of the race, your burning lungs and sheer adrenaline cause your vision to go blurry for a second as you regain your breath and your heart starts to slow down and recover. At that point, I saw one light on the block in front of me. I looked around at the other lanes and realised I was the first at the wall. Less than a second later, the others came in after me. I remember hooking onto the block with my left arm and turning around to look at the results board. My vision was still not focusing properly and it took what seemed like ages to realise that the number 1 was by my name and that my time had broken the European record. At that point, incredulation and pure shock took over. Getting out of the pool, rambling on and making no sense in my media interviews and stumbling around to the pool, I met the coach who had spoken to me before I went out. He looked at me slightly bemused, because I think he realised that I had no idea what had happened. When the gold was hung around my neck, I didn't cry, I was still in shock. It was only the next morning on my day off, I met my family in private and the sheer enormity of the moment hit me. The floodgates opened and when I finally realised what had happened, I couldn't stop crying. That moment was a lesson for me. As cheesy as this sounds, I really understood that the unexpected can happen and that life holds plenty of delightful surprises, as well as challenges, all of which are designed to thrill and test us in equal measure. It was pure magic.

ELITE INSIGHT

John Jackson –
Sochi 2014 Olympics Bronze Medallist, Bobsleigh

I remember watching the news in December 2016 when the McLaren report released its findings about the Sochi 2014 Winter Olympics and how there had been a Russian state sponsored doping programme throughout.

Initially we didn't understand who was involved, how it affected us and what would happen to the result. At first it was disbelief that this level of cheating had happened during my final Olympic Games. This was shortly followed by disappointment and frustration that we may have been cheated out of standing on an Olympic podium. Originally, we had finished fifth just 0.11 seconds out of the medals with two Russian sleds in front of us. Out of the eight Russians in the two sleds, one had a banned substance in his system, five more were found to have samples tampered with. Though the appeals process and waiting for the final decision was frustrating, that built into pure joy when we found out they had been found guilty of anti-doping rule violations.

In May 2019 I was called by the British Olympic Association, to inform me our result at the Sochi 2014 Winter Olympics had been upgraded from fifth to third and we would retrospectively receive our medal later in the year. This decision came as relief, more than any other emotion. It had been such a mentally frustrating journey to get to that stage. In November 2019, five years and ten months after the event, we were awarded our medal.

I retired in the middle of 2016 from the sport of bobsleigh, but felt like I'd never been able to fully walk away. Becoming an Olympic Medallist and the presentation of the medal, allowed me to close that chapter of my life.

When you're at a competition, no matter how important or how much more pressurised it is, don't change your routine. Learn what works for you and stick to it.

Remember reading about how well it worked for me when I ignored what all the other competitors were doing? Yep, that was next on my list of things to do to maximise my performance. I didn't want to know what times the other girls were getting or how it might affect what I did. That's fine in theory, but at the Olympics there's an enormous tannoy, blasting out commentary on each athlete as they're about to do their run. Then there's the beep system that tells the athlete when to start their run, followed by a running commentary and ending with the time they'd achieved.

I'd decided on using a hugely sophisticated, technologically advanced technique to avoid knowing anything that was happening outside. I stuck my fingers in my ears and hummed loudly! I knew that whatever time they'd got, it wasn't going to change my performance.

Your competitors have no bearing on what you can achieve.

I did all of my warm-ups in that room as well. I knew the ideal body temperature I wanted to achieve, based on all the years of training and competing, so inside my coat I had my foil blanket on to trap in the heat, I had my hot water bottle, I was getting my muscles warm in exactly the same way I did for every competition.

Emphasise proper warming up, all the time, both to maximise performance and avoid injury.

Everything in that room was based on me not getting overwhelmed by the whole experience. It was my safe and happy bubble and it was precisely what I needed.

THE RUN

Finally it was my turn. I came outside for my final run, with absolutely no knowledge of how everyone else had done. I didn't know if anyone had crashed, had done a super-fast run or a super slow run. I only had thoughts of myself and what I was going to do.

I had everything ready, all my kit was on, warm-ups done, normal routine done. I walked out to the starting point, still wrapped up in my foil blanket to maintain temperature. My coach, Mickey Grunberger, was with me, carrying my sled (Arthur). I was wearing a darkened visor and remember a very tiny moment of eye contact with Mickey. I remember looking across at Woody, my other coach who just gave me a quick nod. Between Mickey, Woody and myself, we just got a sense of "oh my goodness, here we go". At the same time, because of my preparation and everything I'd done in the build-up (for years!), there was a sense of peace and calm. Mickey patted me on the back and just said something simple, "right, here goes". It was like a comfort blanket of confidence. We've got this.

I'm then listening for the clock, waiting for the countdown to begin. I hear the safety buzz to say the track is all clear and safe, then as soon as I see the red light turn to green, I had to whip off my foil blanket and salopettes as fast as possible, get into my start position with my sled, and start sprinting as soon as possible. I knew that I had in the region of six seconds before my body lost its optimal performance temperature.

Remember when we discussed attention to detail in the training and preparation chapter? Because of this, I'd gone to the point of sewing Velcro down the side of my salopettes, across my shoe protectors and down the front of my coat, so I could whip them all off quicker and not lose a second of body temperature.

Remember the importance of details.

At this stage I was trying so hard to solely concentrate on the run. I tried not to look at anyone or anything. It's incredibly difficult to maintain this blinkered focus and I remember suddenly becoming aware of the camera pointing directly at my feet, filming the start. In the split second of distraction caused by the camera, I noticed my back foot was shaking like a leaf and the camera was zooming right in on my feet. I instantly thought about the people watching me through their TV thinking how nervous I must be with my shaking foot. I recognised the thought process immediately and a switch went off in my mind. Right, focus, stop thinking, get into position, remember your technique, drive the knees forward and "eat the ground".

Recognise whether or not your thought process is helpful to your performance. If it isn't, use positive affirmations, refocus.

The difficulty of preparing for an event like the Olympics is that no matter how much preparation, how much mental and physical training you do, you simply can't replicate the environment. If it wasn't the camera momentarily taking my focus, it was the big crowds, the cowbells clanging and the crazy buzz around the whole track. I didn't know in advance whether the closeness of the crowds to the track would be a distraction while I was sliding. It was impossible to completely blank it out, as much as I tried.

Plan for every possible situation that you can, but make sure you have mental flexibility for things you can't plan for. Control the controllables.

The red light then turns green. My focus was all on technique. Explode into the sprint, get into that perfect body position. This takes me back to day one of my life in skeleton. The very first lesson I was ever taught on ice: "here's the perfect body position, head down, shoulders down and feet together". Seems quite strange that eight years after that first session, here I was sprinting out at the Olympics thinking about the first thing I was ever told.

Drill your fundamentals; listen to coaches; listen to those more experienced than you.

It's such a steep start at the Whistler track that very quickly the first corner comes into view. It's a really tough one: it's aggressive, short and sharp and really whips you around hard to the right, immediately piling on the g-force. It was so important to get that first corner correct so you and your sled are in position for the second turn that comes along quickly as well. Coming out of corner 3 I was already at around 50 mph, so now it was time to get into the sliding flow and rhythm after such an aggressive start. Getting through these next corners was a big moment, I was settling down, feeling natural and comfortable. I could refocus again, think about each corner and rely on all the track preparation, mental imagery and all the techniques I'd learnt.

Preparation isn't just physical, for any sport. Do your homework on every aspect of the challenges in front of you.

Corners 4 and 6 were the next big corners; these were tough ones where you have to get the pressures right. As your sled goes into a corner, the g-force sticks you to the track and the pressure will want to drive you upwards on the slope (convex) of the track. I needed to steer the sled with my shoulders (and sometimes feet) at exactly the right moment so it's at the correct angle when that pressure hits. With a margin of error of only a couple of centimetres at such high speeds, the only thing I had to rely on was endless years of detailed training. It comes down to feelings, your peripheral vision and senses. I'm now travelling at 60–70 mph.

Train hard and performance comes naturally.

The metal runners of a sled that are touching the ice are cut in an extremely precise shape, almost like a knife, with only one or two centimetres of them actually touching the ice when you lay on your sled. There's a very unique and specific balance point of a sled when you lie on it, so that you can have the right amount of runner connecting to the ice and have optimal control and balance over your sled. The design allows the sled to pivot in the middle which helps with the steering. If everything isn't perfectly designed and perfectly aligned, then there's no chance of a good run. The science behind them is mind boggling and the team behind my sled (which was only a prototype at the Olympics!) included people like Rachel Blackburn and James Greenwell, two very talented research and development engineers.

Trust your team members to do their job and have them trust you to do yours. Maintain any equipment you have to the highest standard. Get into good habits.

The way corner 6 was designed, there's a split second where you could actually leave the ice entirely and are essentially in flight! You then had to land in the perfect position, get into the right place for the next tricky corners, 7, 8 and 9, that to the naked eye look pretty straight but were more like a chicane on a car racing track. You simply couldn't skid in that area, or it's game over. I had to really sink and relax into the sled and stay as still as possible, despite the enormous explosion of nervous energy coursing through my body at that point on the track. This section of the track I was travelling between 70 and 85 mph.

You're not nervous; you're excited.

The last few corners were just so fast, corners 13, 14, 15, 16 it was bang bang bang and you were at the end, with a mass of g-force coming with you. You're trying to look ahead as far as you can, but the g-force is pinning your head to the ice and it takes every ounce of strength to keep your head and body in a good position at just over 90 mph.

Eat well, sleep well and prepare your body in the smartest way possible for the challenges you'll face.

Coming out of the very last corner, everyone, including me, hit the wall, it was impossible to avoid. This is where I had a bit of luck being one of the lighter girls in the event. Sometimes you want to be heavier so gravity takes you down the track faster, but on the flipside, the heavier athletes would hit the wall harder and this bled their speed more.

You'll need a bit of luck occasionally.

Then it's just head down, get over the finish line as quickly as possible, gradually coming out of the "zone" of competing and thinking more about stopping (no breaks on a sled!). So I was up on my elbows, slowing down and stopping with the help of lots of broken ice and snow chucked on the track and a big pile of foam matting at the end. It was done, albeit in a slightly ungraceful manner with a load of foam on top of me.

I remember the crowd at this point, cowbells and cheering creating a huge wall of noise. I had literally no clue the position I'd finished in. Yes the crowd were going crazy, but it was the

Olympics; that's just what they do. Even as I was getting off the sled, I was immediately critical of myself. I'd made some mistakes: there'd still been some corners that I hadn't perfected, even though it was the Olympic final.

Perfection isn't possible; do the absolute best you possibly can; be kind to yourself and always look for those 1% gains in everything you do.

I didn't want to presume I'd won at this stage. I knew I'd had a lead going into the final run, but I was also acutely aware that I'd never won a race and had only ever been "training champion". I didn't know how the other girls had done, I didn't know if any of the mistakes I'd made had been enough to erase my lead.

I stood up off the sled, helmet balanced on my head and my face poking out, completely in the dark as to what had happened. One of the coaches, Andi Schmidt, who later went on to become performance director, was at the bottom of the track, knowing I'd won before I did. He came over and hugged me, slapping my back excitedly. I simply asked him, "Where did I finish?". I don't think I'll ever forget his response:

"You're Olympic Champion".

Persevere.

If you look at the video on YouTube, I then suddenly start slapping his back equally excitedly and that's the point I knew. I remember thinking, "Okay, what on earth do I do now?!" I'd never actually visualised myself winning, my concentration had always been entirely on my process goals. If I do everything right, then the results will take care of themselves. I'm afraid my visualisation techniques had failed me on this occasion as I had no idea what to do after actually winning.

Concentrate on the process, not the outcome.

When it started to sink in, I began to realise what had happened. It was thrilling to see two of my closest friends on the circuit, Anja Huber and Kerstin Szymkowiak, getting second and third so I could share the moment with them.

Sport brings you wonderful friends and so many benefits beyond simply winning.

Someone then threw me a union jack from the crowd. I'm not certain but it may have come from a group of half-naked guys, with "Amy" spelled out on their chest; do let me know if you ever know who it might have been! In hindsight, I wish I'd unfurled it slightly more gracefully and neatly so I could hold it up like I saw Sally Gunnell do all those years ago that inspired me so much. But no, it was a bit of a crumpled mess. I was so aware of everyone staring, shouting and cheering; I was still this shy girl from Bath and I didn't quite know how to react.

Never place limitations on yourself because you think your personality might not be right for elite sport.

I knew my parents were somewhere at the bottom of the track and I was trying to see them in the crowd. It was mayhem, I saw my dad from afar, but apparently my mum was attempting to make her way through the crowds to see me and I couldn't see her. I also just wanted to hug Micky Grunberger, but he was at the top of the track for the start so I couldn't get to him either. There was a weird sense that everyone I wanted to hug weren't close enough to grab!

Take comfort from those closest to you, they know you better than anyone and are your biggest supporters. Appreciate them.

Thankfully I just kept getting whisked away to different areas.
I had to do the formalities of putting myself and my sled on
the scales – there are strict weight restrictions and rules of the
sled and then the added weight of the athlete. Then there
was a quick flower ceremony which was lovely to share a
moment with Anja and Kerstin. Then it's off into the media
zone and a first interview with Clare Balding. Clare being
Clare hit me with a load of very well researched statistics
that I was the first British Winter Olympic gold medallist for
30 years and first female individual gold medallists in 58 years. I
hadn't thought about these things before at all (it's those process
goals again). I was just more amazed at being interviewed by
THE Clare Balding …! Someone had told me that even Sir Richard
Branson was there at the bottom of the track cheering me on with
the rest of Team GB, although in the madness I didn't get to see him.

After that, it's back to more normality, putting on the warm
clothes, and needing to find a fresh water bottle that hadn't been
opened so I could start drinking it in preparation off weeing in
a pot for the drugs testing that is standard for the top 3 finishers
and a further 3 random competitors. Someone had managed
to find my parents at this point, they had been chaperoned to
the bottom of the track in the car park where the Bobsleigh
containers were kept. That was yet another special moment, real
hugs with my number one supporters, with policemen, security
and the drugs lady (she never leaves your side until the deed is
done!) all watching on.

I couldn't celebrate properly until I could wee, so eventually off I
go with the drug testing lady off to the testing area.

The feelings then turned to a huge amount of relief (for the
medal, not the wee!). It was an accumulation of a lifetime of
work, but more specifically that four-year period since the Turin

disappointment where I made that conscious decision to make every aspect of my life a positive force towards a set goal.

To know that every day, every hour, every minute had been utterly worth it was just incredibly special. I'd done it. I always knew I could; I always had a sense that if I did the work and showed the total dedication required, then I can do this.

That was my moment, it had to happen there and every race had been leading to that point. It was a result of this quiet confidence within the team of "if I execute everything properly, it's gonna happen".

At this point I was just exhausted. The emotional energy of the weeks leading up to the games, the holding camps, the training, the track walks, everything. I wanted to hug my loved ones, my family, my coaches, the support team, then just sit down and have a cup of tea. It's time like this that seeing friendly faces was the nicest thing. I went back to the Team GB accommodation and the staff were just lovely. Seeing people like Jan Patterson who'd become a second mum during the Olympics, Sir Clive Woodward was there too and it was just a really special environment and feeling.

Getting back to my room, there was a sign on my door with a picture saying "Amy Williams GOLD". Rachel Blackburn, the sled designer, and Chris Price, one of the physios, had bought me a stuffed bear "Quatchi" who was the mascot of the Olympics (who eleven years later currently resides in my young son's bed). It was those little moments that made everything so special and I'll always appreciate and remember them.

That evening I was taken out by various Olympic dignitaries, from the British Olympic Association and Team GB committee members. This was nice; although I was so tired I just wanted to be with my close friends, having something like a McDonalds from the Olympic Village, a meal that I hadn't allowed myself to eat in years. It was a super fancy restaurant and I could barely read the menu due to exhaustion. I remember going into the loo there and just having a little cry. It was just a release of emotion that I hadn't realised had been building up inside me. I'd been so intensely focused, that I'd just parked it to one side until the time came for it to come out.

There's a time for emotion. Stay focussed when you need to be, then you can let it all out later.

THE MEDAL

The day after was the medal ceremony. During the day there were a lot of interviews, travelling around various radio stations and TV studios. Although I'm enjoying it all, and feeling super special being congratulated by everyone, it was a strange feeling, thinking that I was missing out on watching all the other events and cheer on all the other Team GB competitors. I wanted to be with my team and fellow athletes.

The ceremony was really special though. There were lots of other athletes from different sports all getting their medals at the same ceremony. I was there with Kerstin and Anja and just thinking "how cool is this??" I'll always remember the Black Eyed Peas "I've got a feeling" that was playing in the background before we went out. That'll always be my medal song.

You then wait your turn to go up and of course I'm thinking "please remember the words of our National Anthem". I was scanning the crowd for my parents (couldn't see them!) and coaches and support staff. I was also trying so hard to not get too emotional and I didn't want to cry, so it was actually a small relief that I didn't see my parents because they'd have set me off! It was incredible singing the words "God save the Queen" standing on that top step, 1st place. Having the medal placed around my neck, feeling it, touching it and holding it.

The three of us then just went back into a holding room, slumped on a sofa and stared at our super heavy medals. It was a special moment that we shared and something that only sport could have provided. We text each other every single year on the anniversary of the medal ceremony "Happy Medal Birthday". Micky Grunberger and Danny Holdcroft always text me on that day as well and it means a lot to me.

THE AFTERMATH

It's a strange feeling to have so many years with a sole focus on one moment in time, that you subsequently achieve. I'd simply never allowed myself to imagine life as an Olympic champion. Now it was a reality, there I was, carrying the flag (it's seriously heavy) at the closing ceremony, then being presented with a big posh watch by Buzz Aldrin at an Omega function, flying home first class (first time) with Quatchi sat beside me. Then I was pulled away from the airport and straight off to do "The One Show" on the BBC with my sled.

Getting back to my parent's house was supposed to be a return to some kind of normality, which didn't quite work out that way, when loads of TV trucks and camera crews stretched up the road outside their house. The rest of that week was crazy, with an appearance on the Jonathan Ross show, a civic reception, being awarded the Freeman of the City of Bath and an open top bus parade through Bath with people hanging out of windows and waving their union jack tea trays!

ATHLETE IN FOCUS

Helen Glover MBE –
London 2012 and Rio 2016 Olympic Champion, Multiple World and European Champion, Rowing

My first time standing on top of the Olympic podium was an out of body experience. I was up in the crowd looking down at this girl who looked like me having a gold medal put around her neck. I felt it was happening to someone else, and in the weeks following that it just couldn't have been me it had happened to! Some of that was probably down to my route into the sport. Four years beforehand, I barely knew the sport existed, had never sat in a rowing boat before, and was at the end of my training to be a PE teacher. I was identified by the Sporting Giants program and fast tracked into rowing … but no one (including me) thought I'd develop fast enough to make the London Olympics. So to turn up at a home games, as hot favourites … and win … it was beyond surreal.

Everyone else took a big holiday; many on the team retired; others lost their hunger for the sport. I was back in the gym the next day. It took me six months to admit to myself that I was Olympic champion, to come to terms with the fact that this was my reality and life would never be the same again.

Rio was very different. Heather and I had been unbeaten in five years & came into the Games with the full weight of expectation upon us. Steve Redgrave and John Inverdale in the launch BBC broadcast from the games were asked to identify their number one picks for Gold. They both said me and Heather. Steve Redgrave said he'd bet his house on us winning. That obviously came with a whole different set of pressures and terrors. Our first qualifying race was probably our closest we'd had in the whole Olympic cycle. With all that unbearable pressure, this time our win was the release of the pressure cooker. On the Rio podium, all the pent up emotion was released. We were worthy winners, and this time we knew it, and instantly embraced it. The post-victory parties were … well, wild!

FINAL THOUGHTS

Sport is incredible, no matter what level you take part. Everyone from elite athletes to serious club competitors, fun runners, Saturday morning footballers, fitness enthusiasts, crown green bowlers, people just beginning their sporting journey, those that have been involved their whole lives and everyone else in between. The benefits are endless. Your health, your fitness, your social life, your mental health, the life lessons, the fun, the challenges, the progress, the confidence, the list goes on.

I hope this book has inspired you, whichever sport you do or are thinking of doing (do it, do it now), you might find you have a talent for it. If you do, go turn it into a triumph.

I wish you the very best of luck with it – although having read this book, you know you make your own luck, right?

Anything is possible.